1

Designing a Sales Compensation Plan; How to create an effective incentives program for your sales force

All the technical components and practical advice to design, administer and communicate a sales incentives plan that increases productivity and eliminates dissatisfaction.

Title Page

Designing a Sales Compensation Plan; How to create an effective incentives program for your sales force

All the technical components and practical advice to design, administer and communicate a sales incentives plan that increases productivity and eliminates dissatisfaction.

By Vangelis Sakelliou

This book is a collection of white papers written for the technical part of the sales incentives program design process. It gives certain details and guidance how one shall design a scheme and which technical features shall be reviewed, assessed and used. Designing a plan is a challenging process requiring knowledge, experience and certain skillset. This is the right material one needs to use prior to considering implementing a new incentives system or altering an existing one.

In partnership with C4S Consultants Limited, a Sales Compensation and Incentives Scheme Consultancy, www.comp4sales.com

C4S Consultants is dedicated to help sales organisations to achieve their sales objectives by designing a sales incentives scheme that makes sales people achieving their potential.

Contents

9

About This Book

This book has been created with one goal only; to help sales management to understand the importance of motivation schemes to sales people and the principles of designing a sales incentives scheme from its technical terms to its operational and administration aspect.

Sales management understands that the consequences of a scheme designed improperly are negative and may lead to unfortunate circumstances. This book is helping design teams and sales management to avoid making these mistakes and trying to help them design a system that is effective from the beginning.

Many people overlook that the design process involves many different decisions, from considering the sales roles that shall be rewarded and the employees eligible to get incentives for their job and successes to the decision on the target cash compensation for a role, how much of it shall be in variable and how much in fixed salary. The process requires an examination on whether to use a commission or a bonus scheme and why. It also needs to determine what type of goals shall the scheme incentivise and what is the weight for each measure. The book also includes vital information on additional aspects of the program that some people forget to consider such as its administration, operation and communication to the sales force.

The book is the combination of fourteen white paper; these are technical articles that can help one to understand how sales motivation schemes work and how to design an effective one.

Introduction: How Sales Incentives Schemes Work And Why They Matter

Incentives schemes are at the heart of sales management. When designed well, an incentives scheme becomes a tool that can be used to manage, nurture, motivate, and guide a sales team. When the scheme works correctly, it helps the sales team to thrive.

Sales is built around objectives. Nothing is left to chance – there are always objectives and targets to be met. These targets give salespeople a clear path to follow. They ensure that each salesperson knows their objectives, and can form a strategy for success.

The incentives scheme lets salespeople know what reward they can expect if they reach their targets. It's a motivator – that's its core function.

Incentives Schemes Help Organisations Beat The Competition

Organisations today are in the midst of an unprecedented era of harsh competition. They're looking to beat the competition and stand out in sometimes over saturated markets. Consistent sales is the only way to reach the desired revenues and growth – and for consistent sales, you need a reliable sales incentives scheme, among other things.

Consistent sales is a multi-faceted concept. To reach the desired outcome, companies need a quality product or service, with an engaged audience, and the right marketing and placement. They also need an efficient sales force, because no matter how good the product, if the talent isn't there to sell it, the revenue won't come.

Sales Incentives Schemes Are Part Of A Bigger Picture

The ultimate task of a sales department is to uncover both obvious and more hidden problems and needs, that they can solve. A tightly constructed research phase and marketing campaign can create a desire for change, and offer a solution that customers will love.

There are different ways to train salespeople to accomplish their tasks. As well as field experience, sales team productivity can be materially helped by:

- Coaching
- Internal training on the product
- Increasing understanding of the industry and trends
- Working with external sales efficiency consultants
- Direction from management
- Delving into articles and books

The above elements plus the right sales motivation scheme can function side by side to increase sales team productivity and make sure a company reaches its targets.

The Positive and Negative Sides Of Sales Compensation Schemes

A sales compensation scheme motivates salespeople to not only meet their targets, but to exceed them and give their best. The ultimate aim of such a scheme is to bring about both personal and entrepreneurial growth and success. It's easy to see why this is a good thing for individuals and for their employer.

However, incorrect deployment of a sales scheme can have a negative effect on sales. Companies often don't realise quickly enough that there's a problem in the system. To be effective, a sales scheme needs to have the following attributes:

- Affects productivity in a positive way.
- Is well designed to bring about the required results.
- Has been tweaked to fit with the specific goals and distinctive principles of the company.
- Motivates salespeople to make the extra effort.

When done right, compensation plans can steer a company all the way to its goals. From personal experience I can say that in principle they work, but in practice they need to be structured, planned and implemented correctly in order to succeed.

In this paper, we'll look at the psychology behind being part of a sales team, and how sales incentives schemes motivate sales team members. Armed with that understanding, we'll examine how to avoid pitfalls and implement a sales scheme that does what you need it to do.

The Importance Of The Sales Force

It's no exaggeration to say that for businesses who want to survive and thrive by selling a product, their sales force can make or break them.

From a tiny tech start up to a mid-sized advisory firm to a giant multinational bank, every company is looking to sell something. It might be a product, a service, or even an idea. Whatever it is, companies need sales to grow their reach, make profits, and succeed in their goals.

Sales is one of the most fundamental activities in any organisation. Any employee is essentially selling their skills and experience to their employer, whether they're on the sales team or not. Managers sell their ideas to their team. CEOs sell their vision for the company to the shareholders.

The Sales Force: An Invaluable Asset

All employees are valuable assets to their employer. Salespeople are priceless, because they are the front force of a company and it relies heavily on the revenues they bring. Even if a product is of the highest quality and priced in a way the market will bear, it won't sell unless a skilled sales force is on hand to sell it.

With the increased development of digital marketing and alternative sales channels, a wider range of departments have a part to play in revenue generation. Some companies use a traditional sales channel, while others use alternative channels such as focusing on their website, especially if they don't have the time or resources to develop a big sales department. Some companies are very product centric, while others are more customer centric, or run a consultative business.

Whatever the nuances, the fact remains that if a company has a sales team dealing with client requests and focusing on bringing results, that team is invaluable.

Leading The Sale Force

The leadership of the sales force is the responsibility of the head of sales that is accountable for overall revenue generation. They're the one who strategizes the activities of the sales force, and builds a short and long term plan. They have ultimate responsibility for overseeing the total sales structure.

As a leader, they stand as an example to their sales team, and are responsible for coaching and motivating them. They're accountable to both their team, and to the CEO, whose targets and expectations they must meet.

Now we're reminded of the importance of a motivated sales team, let's take a closer look at sales as a profession today.

Sales As A Profession Today

What Makes A Salesperson?

I recently met with a friend who was about to get involved in the sales process for the first time. I told her the truth – that becoming a salesperson is not an easy step, especially if you're not used to it. Even seasoned salespeople find doing such a constantly customer-facing job and persuading them to buy, difficult at times. But why do people find sales so hard?

Sales Requires Constant Communication With Prospects

The answer lies in the definition of the role and its main tasks. **A salesperson needs, above all else, to be good at talking to people**. You can't sell anything if you don't interact with your clients! That means that to succeed, salespeople need to find, target, and contact leads. The prospecting process is the only way to create sales opportunities.

For example, let's look at a B2B company, such as a financial software business. Their product isn't going to show up on supermarket shelves. So, finding and communicating with new clients is essential. Marketing and inbound activity can be effective, but that doesn't negate the need for outbound marketing and human interaction. Even inbound leads will mostly likely end up talking to a salesperson at some point.

These aren't short communications, either. They often continue for months in the pursuit of closing the contract. This process requires constant interaction with the prospective client.

Salespeople Need To Develop This Skill

I've heard of salespeople sweating before a call, dreading talking to that client. Those people find it hard to work in sales, and are unlikely to perform as well as their managers would like.

However, the ability to be good at talking to people is a skill that can be learned, just like any other. Yes, there are some people who seem to have a natural talent for talking to people, but those of us who don't have that inborn talent, can develop it. Developing sales skills can turn even a passive and reluctant salesperson into an active and successful member of the team.

Being an effective salesperson is a learned skill.

Salespeople Must Learn To Navigate Emotions In A Grounded Way

Like any other person, a salesperson is affected by their emotions, and by what's happening around them. Personal factors such as family issues can have a destructive effect on the sales process, being that the process is already an emotional one. Of course, sales is a skill and logic and good planning are needed. But it's helpful for sales managers to always take into account the feelings that the sales cycle brings up, too:

- The nerves or stress before making a sales call.
- Worry about the negative effect on the process if the call goes poorly.
- Tension while waiting to see the results of a call, or an email campaign, or other marketing.
- Frustration when a cold-call client rejects the call.
- The mix of excitement and nerves while waiting for a client to respond to a proposal.

These feelings can get very intense as the sales cycle builds.

Having a lot of emotion around the sales process is perfectly normal. After all, any two people in an interaction have feelings! The body language, tone of voice, and words chosen in a meeting between salesperson and client belie a host of underlying feelings. All sales processes end in either an acceptance or rejection of an offer, so a certain amount of emotion is inevitable.

Salespeople face the unknown every day, and thus need to be prepared for any circumstances. The more salespeople can learn to stay grounded through it all, the easier their jobs will be, and the better they'll perform. Staying calm regardless of the outcome helps a salesperson move on to the next sales case, and the next. Being able to live with the emotions that come up and not be too swayed by them helps salespeople keep their momentum going and their motivation high. Managers who understand and support this are ultimately helping their company achieve its aims.

The Inherent Challenges Of The Sales World

Keeping The Sales Team Motivated

Keeping salespeople motivated is a major challenge for sales managers. It takes considerable time and effort to coach salespeople, train them, and improve their skills. Developing a sales department is not easy, especially because managers need to keep their teams constantly motivated. To better motivate a team, it helps to understand what motivates salespeople.

What Motivates A Salesperson?

What motivates a salesperson? What gets them up in the morning? Is it money, fame, or an appetite for success?

The basic need to survive drives people to have a paid job or their own business – after all, we all need money for necessities.

Effective salespeople are motivated by more than just the necessities. They have the drive to meet and over perform their goals. Motivation can take several forms:

- The satisfaction of reaching a new goal

- The feeling of accomplishing tasks

- Increasing the amount of money earned

- Seeing the company they work for grow

- Winning new customers

- The satisfaction of renewing existing contracts

- The feeling of accomplishment that comes from establishing trust with a client – enough that they're ready and happy to sign a contract

- Beating the competition

Motivation is a personal force, and it's often driven by the need to grow, and to help things grow. For example, the parents of a new-born are excited about their child's growth, which in turn encourages them to support their child and find new ways to help it grow and find fulfilment. In business, this means knowing that success equals more opportunities to grow one's career, such as to move into a better or higher paid role, or even a more senior management position.

Blocks To Motivation

Motivation isn't something to take for granted. External factors can have a serious impact on motivation. These include personal challenges or negative circumstances, such as a difficult home life, or a toxic company culture.

Using Competition Wisely

We live in a competitive world. People compete against each other in many aspects of life, from a pub quiz to a sporting event to friendly rivalry at a family board game night. Competition is, of course, a huge driving force when it comes to sales.

Competition is a powerful tool that can be used to push people to reach and over perform their targets. The sales environment makes it easy to compare the performance of different salespeople. The numbers are readily available that allow managers to compare yearly achievements and commissions earned.

The competition within a company can be fierce. Salespeople don't just want to meet their targets – they want to outperform their colleagues. They're hungry to prove to their management and their colleagues that they can do better, win more clients, and earn more money.

Motivation Schemes Encourage Competition

The very existence of a motivation scheme points to the fact that sales is a competition. Two salespeople with the same skill set might get the same basic salary, but the commission they bring can dramatically change the amount of take-home pay they actually receive.

Companies, obviously, use this to stir their sales team to achieve more. Sales rallies and special incentives further enhance the competition. I've worked for and with several companies where the top three to five salespeople get an extra bonus, or the very best performers win a luxury trip or entry to the President's Club.

A motivation scheme makes it easy for management to compare team members and make decisions. They can easily run a report and see the commissions and performance of each member of the team during a specific time period. It provides an easy way to compare salespeople who have different personalities and skills, because the data can be boiled down to the basic facts: How well did they perform, and what commissions were they paid.

Competition is clearly a good thing in a sales environment. However, it's important to use competition wisely as the line between healthy and toxic competition can be surprisingly thin.

It's common to see sales ranking tables used to motivate the team, or for management to send out an end of year email showing who made quota, and who didn't.

Salespeople naturally want to see their name on the top of the list. Pursuing a sales opportunity needs constant commitment and dedication. Being in winning mode absolutely helps with this. However, managers need to exercise caution and make sure that their team isn't using aggressive sales tactics when they're not called for. For example, when selling a complex solution to a client, sales staff need to play the long game rather than sell aggressively. Managers should keep this in mind and make sure the competitive aspect enhances, rather than damages, sales performance and revenues.

Navigating The Changing Business Landscape

Another challenge inherent in the sales environment is the need to navigate the changing business landscape.

The Role Of Technological Innovation

Technological innovation has helped business in many ways, but there is one downside: Increased competition. For example, a local business these days isn't competing only with other local businesses, but with similar businesses around the world. A shop might have a better product range than another similar shop in the same town, but it also has to compete against online shops (including big players such as Amazon and Ebay.)

For many consumers, cost is the first consideration. If they can buy the same thing cheaper online, they will!

The Investment Space

Companies need to constantly think far into the future, and strategize their plans proactively. They know that their shareholders and investors will constantly monitor the growth of any company they have a stake in. They want to know that if they put in the funding, they can expect results. Analysts evaluate companies not only for historical trends and current growth, but for future outlook.

Investors are naturally keener to put money into companies that have a history of over performing and getting excellent results.

These ongoing challenges posed by both technology and the needs of investors make for a more challenging competitive landscape than ever before. Companies these days need to put in extra effort to not only survive, but to grow fast enough to beat the competition, and attract and keep investors.

Playing The Numbers Game

Sales is at base a numbers game. Numbers are powerful – we use them to compare various companies, even those in different industries and sectors. The numbers are a major factor in whether or not an investor is willing to explore an opportunity.

They'll examine the numbers and use that analysis to decide whether the outlook of the company is good, or not.

Investors always undertake a thorough analysis before making any announcement. There are dozens of different numbers that a company announces and various other KPIs (Key Performance Indicators) that are in place to show the performance of the firm. By standardizing the KPIs that are given in public among different periods, people are able to compare companies and conduct further analysis.

For salespeople and managers, it's a numbers game too. Managers monitor how revenues change between periods, and compare revenues between analogous periods over different years. If the numbers are growing, that means the firm is healthy and developing. Salespeople are given numbers in the form of targets, and their performance is evaluated according to whether or not they meet the assigned quota. Numbers are used to compare the performance of salespeople and teams.

The danger of playing the numbers game is that companies and individuals can get so caught up in quantitative rather than qualitative measures that they put all their focus on the numbers and ignore the quality of the work. This can impact the long-term vision of the firm, and can even negatively affect customer relations. A salesperson who is hungry to meet targets in a period where there are no promising deals might adopt a desperate and unethical approach to sales.

Sales Compensation Schemes: Expectations and Responsibilities

Understanding the role of expectations and the responsibilities inherent in building a sales compensation scheme helps organisations make their scheme as effective as possible.

To fully understand this, we need to first take a look at why motivation systems work.

Why Motivation Systems Work

Goal setting is part of daily life for many people. For example, one person might want to have their first ten thousand dollars in savings by the age of thirty, while the next person might have a goal of running their own company by the age of thirty-five. Goals are highly individual and frequently change as old goals are met and new ones decided upon.

Setting goals gives us a clear vision of the future we want, and helps us plan ahead and become more self-motivated.

Of course, all of this is also true in the corporate world. I can't think of a single company with no goals or objectives! Just like a person with no goals, a company with no vision will lack passion, vision and planning. This puts its very success and its market share at stake. On the other hand, clear goals can help a company succeed even during adverse market conditions.

Motivation Schemes Inspire Employees To Reach Their Goals

Within the company, employees need goals and objects, too. Distinctive goals help employees stay motivated and inspired as they look for ways to fulfil those goals. Setting objectives helps salespeople become self-motivated, but a wise manager also looks to the role of external motivation in reaching goals – and that's where the sales motivation scheme comes in. In today's tough competitive landscape where salespeople are frequently asked to outperform their goals and put in extra effort, external stimulation can make a big difference.

Incentives Schemes Have Two Main Objectives

An incentives scheme has two main objectives: The first is to **give salespeople a clear goal and show them different ways to meet that goal**.

The second goal is often overlooked. It's easy to assume that a motivation scheme is simply the sum of money paid for performance. However, the motivation scheme also exists to **strengthen the strategy of the company** and help the organisation as a whole reach its corporate goals.

For an incentives scheme to reach both its objectives, it's vital that salespeople understand the underlying purpose and design of the scheme. This is the responsibility of the sales manager.

Sales Incentives Encourage That Extra Step

Having a sales incentives scheme in place encourages sales staff to go that extra step, to reach that goal and outperform it. Although money isn't the only powerful motivating factor in the world, or even in sales, knowing there's a reward to be had for making extra effort encourages staff to put in the extra effort.

Managing Sales Scheme Expectations

Managing expectations is an important part of making sure a sales scheme works as desired. The first expectation to throw out the window is that the scheme must be perfect.

In my years working with sales teams I've learned this: There's no such thing as a perfect motivation scheme. Sales schemes are by their nature complex and there are many factors that feed into their success or lack of:

1. The difficulty of predicting its real-world influence

2. The dynamic nature of most markets

3. The constant shifts in commercial terms, offerings, and even sales methodologies

It's impossible to know for sure whether a sales incentives scheme will match the anticipation of the stakeholders. The best a company can do is stay aware and course correct as necessary.

There are also situations where a motivation system sounds perfect to the management but doesn't actually work for the sales team. Sales managers need to be cautious and be sure that if their amount of paid commissions is on the rise, so too are their revenues. An increase in paid commissions should be aligned with an increase in business. Other pitfalls to look out for include:

- The company failing to reach goals and targets
- Low profit margins

- Inability to land new clients

Managers need to be realistic in their expectations for the sales scheme – and they need to be very clear on those expectations. For example, if the goal is an increase in revenues, there should be a demonstrable correlation between the money paid in commissions and the amount of revenue sales staff bring in. Managers must also take into account different factors: If revenues and commissions are both going up, but profits are going down, that's a red flag.

It's also important that managers don't expect the sales motivation scheme to bear the entire responsibility for the company's success. Some people have tried to argue that using such a scheme creates money-driven personalities that commit to the company for the wrong reasons. I certainly don't agree with this: The ability to earn good commissions is a fantastic motivator. However, it doesn't work that well when it's the only motivator.

Sales staff will find it harder to commit and give their all if the company overlooks the importance of career advancement opportunities, good benefits packagers, and a professional and supportive working environment. All these things support and work alongside the sale scheme to create motivation.

Don't Expect Miracles From Your Sales Scheme

Incentives schemes exist to support the financial and strategic goals of a company, and to align salespeople to the correct direction. However, a sales scheme is not the only management tool available, and managers shouldn't rely on it alone.

Successful sales also require:

- A good product
- The correct marketing
- Building an efficient and skilled sales force

The best motivation scheme in the world can't bring the desired results if there's another piece of the puzzle missing.

For example, if the product is outdated and the competition is several steps ahead, the motivation scheme alone might not be enough to increase revenues. Or, the product might be ideal for the market, but the sales team is lacking the necessary skills to close deals. This can be especially true in the case of new or newly altered sales schemes, when the sales force is still getting to grips with the new system.

A sales scheme is a powerful tool, and it can doubtless be used to change the direction of a sales force and positively affect the mentality of salespeople. However, managers mustn't underestimate the other tools at their disposal to steer the sales force in the desired direction.

Is It Possible To Skip The Sales Scheme Altogether?

In light of this you might be wondering whether it's possible to skip the sales scheme altogether. After all, it comes with a financial cost. Is it possible to inspire a sales force to be committed without using a motivation scheme?

A compensation plan is a sales supporting tool. Sales management uses it to manage the sales force and drive people towards a certain direction. But can effective sales management replace a motivation scheme? Can sales schemes and sales management be used interchangeably, or do they work better in tandem?

How To Define Whether Sales Management Is Effective

How can one measure whether sales management is effective? Is it possible to relate sales results directly to sales management, and further, to how they interact with their team?

Efficient sales management consists of processes and procedures constructed with the aim of reaching set goals and bringing about sales success. Effective sales management motivates the sales team to meet both their daily and longer-term goals.

Good sales management combines outstanding leadership skills with training, coaching and monitoring of the team's activities. Effective management is always in line with the company's culture and ethos, and is thus very supportive to employees.

The Effect Of Size And Complexity On Sales Management

Even a perfectly organized and managed sales environment will have issues when the size of the organisation increases, and the complexity of the sales process surges.

It's been my experience that the size and complexity of the firm has an impact on management efficiency. In a small firm it's easier to manage people and ensure they follow the correct processes. It's much harder to do this in a bigger organisation with many more people. In bigger companies, the leadership program itself takes an injection of time, effort and money, if it's to be designed well.

The Importance Of Sales Support

Compensation schemes are there to pay people for the effort they put in to land and keep customers. In theory then, salespeople who make less effort than their peers to persuade a client to sign, should make less commission.

Part of effective sales management is providing the support sales staff need to enable them to sell. This could include:

- Sales programs and training
- Inside sales support
- Telemarketing
- Marketing campaigns
- Attractive marketing materials

All these can make a difference to how well the team performs – and all these are the responsibility of sales managers to provide.

Effective Sales Management Still Can't Replace A Motivation Scheme

It would be easy to assume, from the above, that so long as the sales management is effective enough, a motivation scheme isn't strictly necessary. However, this is not true. There are other factors to take into account outside of how efficient sales management is, such as market and industry practices, and company goals, all of which impact a salesperson.

In addition, it remains the truth that the role of a salesperson is still hard, even if they have excellent support. They're still responsible for closing deals. Even with good support and top-notch marketing materials, there's no guaranteed win. The salesperson needs a strong strategy, well implemented, to win customers.

Although having no motivation system in place is also a choice, I don't recommend it. If a company is determined to go this route, I'd say through thinking, analysis and a strong decision-making process is a must. However, people are by nature competitive, and sales is a competitive field. Sales staff perform better when they see a clear goal and understand the benefits of reaching that goal. A motivation scheme can help provide those benefits.

Neither a strong motivation scheme nor effective sales management can provide all the answers and results. Rather, it's helpful to have both working in tandem for optimum results and success.

The Responsibilities Of Having A Motivation Scheme

A motivation scheme has the potential to bring terrific results in terms of increasing revenues, meeting goals, and spurring the sales team to greater heights.

However, a sales scheme can also have the opposite effect. If not properly designed, a sales scheme can demotivate people, harm the sales force, and have a dramatic negative impact on the sales numbers and productivity of the company.

There are three pitfalls that managers must be careful to avoid:

- salespeople incorrectly misinterpreting the system (this is often a problem of lack of clear communication from the management).
- salespeople using the system to their advantage when it fits their strengths towards selling certain products, but not using it correctly at other times.
- salespeople noticing that the system hardly adds much to their pay packet, and therefore not engaging with it.

Any of these issues will affect the sales teams' performance and the company's results. Plus, demotivated salespeople are more likely to leave the company for a better opportunity, which means more time and money spent on finding and training new sales staff.

No company can afford to risk its future, so managers must take the level of responsibility that comes with using a motivation scheme seriously. When designing and communicating the system, managers must recognise and accept the responsibility that comes with it, staying aware that motivation schemes can both increase and decrease success.

No company can afford to risk its future and that shows that the level of responsibility behind the notion of motivation plans is quite important.

How To Avoid An Ineffective Sales Scheme

It's clear that companies must avoid designing a scheme that hinders more than it helps. **But how does one avoid that?**

Let's start by looking at some questions a company can ask, to determine if a motivation scheme is right for them.

Deciding If A Motivation Scheme Is The Right Step

Organisations often assume they need a sales motivation scheme, just because everyone else in the marketplace seems to have one. So many companies follow the current trend and market practice of implementing a sales scheme without stopping to ask if it fits their strategy and principles. I have met with many executives who assume that their company needs a motivation scheme just because their competitors do.

The effects of an incentives plan are well known in the business world. A new plan or a few tweaks to an old one can bring about a significant increase in results. An ill-designed plan can lead to the loss of good salespeople.

Even if the benefits are clear, it's good business sense to analyse any decision before jumping in. Before implementing a sales scheme, organisations might ask:

- What do they want to achieve through a motivation system?
- What's the advantage of paying additional commissions on top of salaries?
- What specific value will it add to the business?
- Is there another way to add that value?

- Is the company wanting to use a commission system because everyone else does?
- Are they doing it out of fear of losing salespeople?
- Would a strong system of performance-based promotion work instead?
- How well do managers understand what employees are looking for from their role, and how a commission scheme fits into that?

Asking these questions encourages strategic thought and ensures the decision has been thoroughly considered. Having worked as a salesperson and also as someone who designs motivation schemes, I know from experience that sales motivation schemes work. The trick is in careful design, and in being willing to revisit the existing motivation plan, analyse its efficiency, and not be afraid to tweak and improve it.

Be Realistic About The Time It Takes To Design A Scheme

A sales incentives plan isn't something you can design in an hour. It's not a simple case of deciding the commission rates that each salesperson will get depending on their performance. There is a strict agenda of factors one needs to take into consideration before releasing the scheme to the sales force.

The design process starts with understanding why the company needs the scheme, and what its objectives are. It also needs to include oft-neglected elements such as how the scheme will be administered and communicated. These "smaller" areas might not seem as important – but if you skip over them, the whole scheme could come down.

Decide On Your Metrics For Success

The definition of a sales motivation system varies depending on who you ask. The CFO of an organisation might measure it by the impact of incentive payments as a cost to the business and its profitability. For them, the motivation scheme isn't effective if the gross profit versus the cost of paying incentives is not improving.

On the other hand, the head of sales might say that they don't mind spending more money in the commission scheme once revenues are coming and targets are met.

They'd use any available budget and any sales tool, including costly marketing initiatives, an expensive contact relations management system, or sponsoring events and conferences to raise awareness. To him, cost isn't the only consideration.

The CEO however might be looking for a balance between revenues and costs, and to create a healthy working environment that supports the company's principles. That way he can prove to the shareholders that the value of the company is increasing.

The lesson here is that people in different positions use completely different key metrics to define success and effectiveness. This can lead to internal miscommunication and a lack of alignment of business objectives. Reaching agreement on principles and the definition of effectiveness is vital for the success of a sales motivation scheme. Everyone involved must know the principles and aims, and how those are to be measured.

Look For Quantifiable Information

It's easy to qualify whether or not a system is effective, as the term "effective" can be quantified. By using accessible data and metrics, the team can measure the success of the system. If for example it drives people to bring new deals or to get a certain amount of revenue from a specific industry, that's easy to measure.

However, management needs to stay aware that some successes are not easily quantifiable. For example, winning a small contract with the biggest targeted company might not look like a success in terms of dollars made, but it could be the first step into a long-lasting relationship with a very profitable client.

Once management decides on which performance measures are most important for the company, it becomes easier to quantify the success and efficiency of the system.

Finding Agreement On What The System Should Be Doing Is Vital

If each department was asked to design an effective sales scheme, the company would end up with several very different systems! That's why the working group in charge of sales scheme design needs to have a common approach as to the definition of "effective", and the steps needed to get there. Having too many clashing goals and wants can make the design of an effective plan even more difficult.

In one organisation I worked with, there was a debate over the cost of the sales scheme. Although it had led to a subscription rate for their service that exceeded expectations, it came with a higher cost. Sales and finance couldn't agree on this. Sales was happy with the increase in clients and upfront fees, but finance was not happy with the deteriorating profit margin. They lacked a common approach to setting targets and goals, and prioritizing objectives.

The Purpose Of A Sales Scheme Is Twofold

The purpose of a sales scheme is essentially twofold:

1. To motivate salespeople to meet and exceed their targets.

2. To create a unified sales force that's aligned with the firm's principles and objectives.

This is important. If sales staff are highly motivated but don't comply with the company's ethos and principles, that might have only short-term benefits. I consulted for a technology company that had a highly successful salesperson, with a lone wolf character that meant he didn't gel with the company's culture. Although his efforts brought a short-term increase in revenues, those revenues started plummeting after a few months.

It's not always clear at first just how big of an impact aligning the sales scheme with the company's overall goals and culture has. Of course, there's the chance of increasing revenues, which is important. But it can have other benefits too:

- Increasing profit margins
- Expanding territories
- Landing new customers
- Landing new types of customers and breaking into new markets
- Higher retention rates in the sales team
- Building a loyal and committed sales force
- Developing a spirit of teamwork

- Enhancing the individual business skills of the sales team members

Getting everyone involved to agree that both these metrics – sales figures and aligning with the company culture – are important creates a strong foundation for the sales scheme.

Understanding Indifferent Systems

The risk of designing a system that is indifferent – i.e. one that has no or only limited positive effect on the company's results – is a very real one.

The key clue that a system is indifferent is when it has a very limited impact on the business, or simply doesn't influence salespeople to improve their performance.

Alternately, an indifferent system might improve some areas of the business, but worsen others. For example, a motivation scheme might drive people to increase revenues, but on the other hand drive down the profit margin.

The negative effects of an indifferent system aren't always immediately obvious, but they become clearer as the months pass. A thorough analysis is needed to discover where the inefficiencies are.

The Potential Damage From An Indifferent Sales Scheme

An indifferent sales scheme can harm a business in ways beyond simply not having a good enough impact on profits:

- Indirectly push staff to over-focus on one specific line, thus destroying other product lines.

- Put too much emphasis on landing new clients without increasing revenues or profits.

- Impacting certain performers more than others and thus not incentivizing all salespeople equally.

- Contribute to incorrect target allocation which makes it hard for some salespeople to earn commissions and thus demotivates them.

The Sales Scheme Must Mirror The Company's Strategy

A motivation scheme should mirror a company's strategy, and strengthen it. If it contradicts the strategy, it will have a negative effect on results. Another definition of an indifferent system is one that doesn't affect sales behaviours in such a way as to align them with the strategy of the company.

An indifferent scheme means salespeople are most likely not paying attention to it, not following it, and frequently ignoring targets and commissions. This jeopardizes the revenue stream of the company. If salespeople are not making the extra effort to earn incentives, then the scheme is simply not working.

No Scheme Can Work For Everyone

When analysing a sales scheme, it's important to remember that no system can be effective for every single salesperson in a company. No matter how good the scheme, it's impossible to design one that every last member of the team is aligned with.

That's why managers need to analyse a scheme's efficiency as compared to the average salesperson's behaviour, rather than panicking if a small minority of people aren't getting results from it.

In general, an effective motivation scheme is one that drives each individual to over perform their past results. For example, if a poor performer was consistently achieving sixty percent of their quota, and a new system raises that to seventy percent, that's an improvement. If the positive change was not due to luck or any external factors, then we can credit the positive effect to the motivation system and its impact on that person's performance.

There are of course some people whom no sales scheme can raise to any great heights, which is why managers must measure how the scheme works for the average salesperson, rather than taking one individual failure to mean the system has failed.

The Sales Motivation Scheme Is Unique For Each Organisation

No two organisations are the same, and thus no two sales motivation schemes should be the same, either.

Motivating The Sales Force Is Very Individual

As we've already discussed, the best sales scheme is one that's used in conjunction with other management tools for optimal results. Figuring out how to best motivate any sales force is a very individual endeavour.

Some other factors that contribute to motivating salespeople into staying with their current employer include:

A Stable Working Environment

This is an important first thing to offer any salesperson. Management shouldn't underestimate how much good this can do. Employees are looking to work for a company that gives them security and a clear career path. No one wants to work for a company where the risk of losing one's job is high. Even in high-risk positions with good compensation, a secure environment is appreciated.

Plenty Of Progress

A constantly developing environment in regards to products and services helps employees feel that they're part of an active organisation. Most salespeople thrive in fast moving environments where they can see the progress around them. If they're going to put lots of effort into selling the company's products, they like to see movement in product development.

Employee Benefits

Benefits such as number of days off, perks, private insurance, and private pension schemes are important to employees and are often a big contributing factor in whether or not they accept a position.

These benefits are not rewards – they should be given to all employees equally regardless of their individual success. There should be no link between how much an employee sells, and how many of these benefits they receive. Knowing their benefits are secure encourages sales staff to stay with the company, and gives them the space they need to focus on making those all important sales.

The Chance To Advance

The chance of promotion is another way to increase employee motivation. Unfortunately, many organisational charts these days are flat without much opportunity to climb the career ladder. If promotion isn't possible or easy, employees should at least have the chance to get involved with new projects and initiatives, and to be rewarded for that, whether in monetary terms or in another way.

A Good Basic Salary

Bonus and commissions are a variable part of the total cash payout. Because of this, the basic salary and the chance of earning a higher basic salary, can be highly motivating.

Finding the best way to motivate and encourage a sales team, and deciding which strategies to implement, is a key factor in success. Commissions are an important part of motivation, but they're not the only part. The decision on which benefits to apply should follow the principle and values of the organisation.

How To Create A Personalized Motivation Plan

Now we understand that every motivation plan is highly personal, let's look more closely at how to create a personalized motivation plan that works for the company.

A motivation system is a tool for empowering sales teams and communicating the overall company strategy to them. A sales scheme makes staff aware of the company's interests and aims.

The Sales Scheme Must Be Aligned With Company Plans

An ill-designed incentive system might reflect a different strategy than the board intended, which is why it's so important to make sure the global aims and the sales scheme are aligned.

Sales staff continuously assess the motivation scheme, and they indirectly absorb the various messages about the overall strategy of the company through it. The strategy and the system shouldn't contradict each other!

Managers should look closely at the system to make sure it is indeed personalized to suit the organisation. For example, if the company decides that the main objective is bringing on new clients, but the system best rewards those who renew contracts with existing clients, there's a disconnect. salespeople will see that renewal is the optimum target for sales staff who want high commissions, so they'll focus their efforts on that instead of on landing new clients.

It's not hard to imagine the disastrous consequences of a motivation scheme that doesn't match the main strategy, objectives, values and principles of the company. Once the system has passed along the wrong message, it becomes difficult to change the mentality of sales staff.

How To Start Constructing A Personalized Commission System

Now you understand that each motivation scheme has its own distinctive character, let's start thinking about what it takes to design a personalized commission system, and what specific parameters should be used. In other words, it's time to make it personal.

Always Reflect The Company's Personality

The sales scheme should reflect the company's:

- Style
- Business culture
- Individual objectives
- Long and short term goals
- Long and short term strategies
- What the company considers as a measure of success

A company shouldn't be afraid to innovate and design something that follows its personal beliefs. No matter what the rest of the industry is doing or what kind of scheme the competition uses, the most important thing is that the company's scheme fits perfectly with its principles and aims.

To do this, companies need to start with the big picture first. What is the long-term goal? What is the true reason for having a motivation scheme – what objectives is the company trying to meet? Once you get the long term and big picture stuff pinned down, it's much easier to work on the details of the system.

The One Rule You Should Never Break

There is one rule companies should never break when constructing a motivation scheme, no matter what the objectives of the scheme: **Follow the principles and values of the company**. That includes the historical values, what the company was founded on, and the values that are held dear in the business culture today.

This is the golden rule of creating commission schemes. Yes, even if it turns out that paying commission doesn't match the overall philosophy of the company.

The values a company holds are part of what keeps sales staff loyal. Changing those values in order to fit in a certain type of motivation scheme compromises trust with employees, and once gone that's very hard to get back. Sticking to the company principles helps build a team's spirit and even provides a boost to a company's overall reputation.

Constantly changing a motivation scheme in order to grab a competitive edge might show weakness and lack of confidence. Of course it's ok – and healthy – to assess the scheme regularly and update it if necessary. But it's not healthy to change the scheme over and over, hoping to hit on the magic button that will bring more profits.

Likewise, it's absolutely fine to research what the competition is doing, and strive to keep one's own motivation scheme competitive – but only inasmuch as it jives with company principles.

A Motivation System Sends A Powerful Message

A motivation system gives top management a unique opportunity to pass a message to its team. The sales scheme has a unique power to connect people between various levels in an organisation. In bigger organisations, where frequent direct communication between different levels is more challenging, the scheme can send messages based on its rules and rewards.

A sales scheme motivates, inspires and guides a sales force. It gives managers the chance to explain, directly or indirectly, the logic behind the system. It represents the overall strategy of the company.

Understanding this makes it clear that communication about the scheme is important. This is true both when a new scheme is implemented and when an existing scheme is changed. Managers should explain why a system is set up as it is and, when it changes, why those changes were made. Even better, they should take the opportunity to explain how those changes relate to their overall strategy – and to the principles of the company.

Communication is important during the design process, too. It can be done by email, sales conference, or small group meetings, just so long as it is done. The words should be carefully chosen, and the content of the communication carefully considered.

Consider How Self-Motivated Your Salespeople Are

As we discussed before, there are many factors that affect a salesperson's daily business life. This raises several questions for sales managers:

- How does a salesperson stay motivated and unaffected and able to continue the sales effort even when circumstances have a negative impact on them?
- Should a salesperson rely always on financial motivation to keep going?
- Is it always a commission system that will stimulate a salesperson's motivation?
- Or should professionals and in particular salespeople build their self-motivation
- Should one wait for someone to congratulate them when winning a deal or should they feel self-satisfied?
- Reassurance is surely important but should employees need that to stay motivated?

It's important to find a balance between self-motivation and external motivation. It's natural to be motivated by a scheme – that's why they exist after all – but a dose of self-motivation provides an ideal balance.

Self-motivated people tend to have positive energy and more easily build a winning status. Their overall attitude builds their self-motivation and confidence, which generates even more energy, in a positive cycle.

Self-motivation helps salespeople build staying power in an unstable world. The truth is that if they had plenty of money guaranteed, most salespeople wouldn't think about the specifics of the motivation system! This shows that there are often other motivators, such as the satisfaction of reaching goals, finding clients, or climbing the career ladder, at work.

A sales force motivated solely by commissions and the promise of a reward for meeting goals isn't as strong as one that has a combination of self-motivation and the motivation of the incentives scheme. Building a sales force can be tricky – getting this balance right takes time, but in the long run it can have powerful positive effects.

Critical Points To Consider When Deploying An Incentives Scheme

It's clear by now that designing and deploying an incentives scheme requires careful planning and consideration. Here are some additional points which it's important to keep in mind.

Justifying The Cost Of Commissions

Paying commissions is a considerable cost for any company. Most times this cost counts as an operating expense that has a direct impact on the income statement of the company. These sums can be rather large indeed. As with any other cost, the price of paying commissions should be fully justified (especially in high amounts). Management should be fully aware that the money paid out in commissions is for a good reason, whether that's increase of revenues, or another company objective such as increasing market share.

Being Aware Of Potential Negative Impacts

As we discussed earlier, a poorly designed scheme can have a negative impact on the sales force. Incentives schemes have the power to direct salespeople to a certain sales behaviour, and so having the wrong set of objectives baked into the scheme can lead them in the wrong direction. Once this happens, it's difficult to turn the sales force back to the right path. Doing so requires even more time and money, since now the sales staff have got used to the wrong direction and management has to change their mentality. Good system design and careful consideration of how much is paid and why are critical to staving off such a crisis.

The Effect Of The Sales Scheme On Turnover

When considering how to design a personalized motivation scheme for a company, managers should remember that the sales motivation scheme can have a dramatic effect on turnover. As we talked about above, it takes significant effort and money to find and train new salespeople. As such, it's in a company's interest to keep turnover low. *A fair reward system that gives everyone equal opportunity to succeed can help with this, and a well-designed sales motivation system supports this principle.*

Aligning The Scheme With Customer Needs

Most, if not all, companies today operate on the principle of "customer first". After all, customers are the ones who pay in the money and who have the power to damage a company's reputation if they have a negative experience. salespeople should have a strong focus on promoting the right solution to each client, the one that will give them genuine value. It's important that the motivation system with its rules and terms doesn't encourage salespeople to promote wrong solutions to clients in favour of making bigger commissions. Sales schemes need to support, not contradict, the "customer first" stance.

It's clear that managers should think long and hard before designing a sales motivation scheme. Bearing in mind the consequences of a badly designed scheme is helpful in this case, because it brings more clearly into focus the importance of correct scheme design. This isn't to put managers off from sales scheme design – done well it's an incredibly powerful tool that can have massive benefits to the company. It's simply prudent to keep these vital points in mind both when designing the overall shape of the scheme, and when putting together the smaller details.

The Short And Long Term Benefits Of Deploying A Sales Motivation Scheme

Although there are some alternatives to a sales scheme, as outlined above, the truth is that most companies who sell direct to clients have a sales scheme as either their primary motivator, or as part of the mix.

The reasons for this is of course that there are so many benefits to deploying a sales motivation scheme.

There are drawbacks too, and we've talked about those. If poorly designed a scheme can certainly turn into a de-motivational scheme rather than a motivational one. But let's remind ourselves of some of the main benefits.

Supporting Revenue Generation

However, by their nature motivation schemes are designed to support the revenue generation process of a company. They help managers to quickly and easily build a sales force that is pro-active and involved, and constantly seeking to close as many opportunities as possible. This is a very clear benefit for any company.

Steering The Actions Of Salespeople

Sales schemes can also be used to shift the actions taken by salespeople. For example, if a company launches a new product and is eager to sell it, then the sales scheme can be used to steer the team in the direction of selling that product as a primary goal.

Imparting Strategy

Sales schemes do great double duty as a communication tool between management and salespeople. A well-explained sales motivation scheme helps employees understand the company's strategy, development, and future plans. If the plan correctly mirrors the strategy, then it can be used to incentivize people towards fulfilling that strategy.

Evaluating The Sales Team

Looking at the end of year incentives paid is a clear way to judge who is performing highest. There may be other factors at work too, such as target allocation or having the correct training, but the sales scheme can certainly contribute to employee evaluation.

Over the long term, a motivation scheme has the potential to keep the sales force happy and motivated to bring results, and to stay loyal to the company. The system can also help salespeople stay focused on their main tasks, and create a unified sales force with a strong team spirit.

A system that's properly aligned to the main strategy can both boost revenues and drive the sales force to achieve the strategic needs of the company.

A Powerful Tool For Sales Managers

The role of a sales manager isn't always easy. True leaders need to have the natural skill of influencing and inspiring people to do their best and reach their goals. The sales manager is responsible not only for bringing the required revenues, but for managing the team and keeping them performing at their best. Strong leadership is non-negotiable.

A well-designed motivation system has the power to lead a whole organisation to a different level, making it a perfect complement to the sales manager's interpersonal skills. salespeople are motivated by the potential commission they can earn – and as the CEO or Head of Sales gets to decide the commission levels, they have a lot of power. That includes the power to use the motivation scheme to motivate the team to put in the extra effort and over perform their targets in a way that brings more revenues and leads to a more satisfied sales team, too.

The sales scheme makes it so much easier for sales managers to communicate and pass messages to their salespeople. This keeps communication transparent and makes sure sales teams understand the reason behind the system's design and rules. This in turn unifies the team and strengthens the strategy of the firm.

A Word Of Warning

If not communicated properly, a sales scheme can seem like a punishment that disciplines and penalizes salespeople. For example, if it only pays commissions above seventy percent of target realization, that indirectly sends a message that those who don't make seventy percent or more will be punished. Of course, a sales scheme can't equally reward every player – but sales managers need to stay aware of this aspect, and ensure their communications properly set out the benefits, and the scheme feels more like motivation than punishment.

Many times though, especially if not communicated well, it can be considered as a "punishment" tool that disciplines and penalizes improper tactics. Managers can also use it to drive sales behaviours to certain directions such as selling certain products against others or products with higher profit margin. If for example a motivation system pays commissions only above seventy percent of target realization, indirectly it "punishes" people that don't meet that level and it passes a strong message that it is expected everyone to make at least seventy percent of their targets.

Sales managers should stay aware that they have a powerful tool in their hands that can affect not only sales activity and behaviour, but emotions, too.

Conclusion: Now Is The Time To Take Action

Whether you're about to design a motivation scheme or you need to tweak your existing one, there's no time like the present.

If you don't have a scheme in place yet, now is the time for a thorough analysis of which kind of scheme will work for you and how best to implement it. If you don't, you're potentially missing out on a powerful sales tool.

This is doubly true if your company has a system but hasn't implemented it yet. That's a waste of time and energy – examine it, make sure it's fit for your aims, and make use of it.

If your company has a scheme in place, now might be a good time to analyse the performances and the incentives paid, to make sure everything is working as it should. Perhaps the findings will show that everything is working perfectly and no actions are needed – that's the result all companies want, but it's still better to analyse and find out for sure if that's the case.

If, however, there is an issue, it's better to tackle it sooner than later. For example, if it turns out the system is paying a lot of money for selling a product that has a high negative margin, something needs to change. Or if the system isn't aligned with the main strategy and people are being paid more money for a different product than the one management wants to promote, that's also cause for immediate action.

Major issues like this often require immediate correction. However, sales teams and companies need stability, consistency, and a clear road to follow. It's not a good idea to tweak the system every time a minor fault is found. In general, I recommend undertaking a small calibration if needed every couple of months, and implementing bigger changes more infrequently than that.

Taking no action at all if something isn't right with a scheme, or if there is no scheme at all, is not a good solution. Sales motivation plans can be easily managed and it's a good idea to be proactive about that, to give them the best chance of succeeding.

White Papers

As mentioned a few times already, the process of designing a sales incentives scheme is a technical work. It requires one following a certain process and setting certain terms and conditions. Designing the system does not finish with just deciding the commission a sales person would get for each deal she brings. The design process begins far before this decision and way after deciding that.

The fourteen white papers that follow are carefully written and chosen as they collectively form the entire guidance of the sales compensation scheme design process.

They are also put together in a sequence depicting the thought process one needs to follow to design a scheme.

Consequences Of A Poorly Designed Incentives Scheme – How To Identify Problems And How To Correct Them

Introduction

Every company that sells products or services wants to increase their revenue without pushing their expenses up too high. A sales motivation scheme is one of the key ways a company can maximize their earnings. Of course, a motivation scheme does mean making payments too – after all, sales people are there to earn a living! That's why an efficient scheme matters so much. An efficient and well-designed scheme means the best return possible for the investment.

Even in cases where sales targets are challenging, the right scheme can work magic and cause a rise in revenues.

Is A Sales Scheme Worth The Expense?

There's no short answer to this. Sometimes it is, and sometimes it's not. It all comes down to how well designed the scheme is. Regardless of the exact mechanics of the scheme, it needs to be properly planned and executed if it's to be effective.

Let's take a closer look at the issue of inefficient sales motivation schemes, and what to do about them.

The Dangers Of An Ineffective Sales Motivation Scheme

The primary objective of any sales incentive scheme is to increase productivity and make sure the sales strategy and company aims are in line. A sales scheme tells the sales force what is expected of them, and the rewards they can expect in turn for meeting targets.

However, if the scheme isn't well-designed, a company can soon suffer the negative effects. An ineffective scheme poses a significant threat to the future and finances of the company. Some of the dangers of an ineffective sales scheme include:

- The scheme doesn't influence sales people correctly, so they don't reach targets.

- The scheme doesn't have a positive impact on sales, and as a result the company's profit suffers.

- The scheme doesn't send the right messages to the sales staff, and as a result they simply ignore the message management is trying to convey.

- The scheme is too complicated, so sales people can't correctly follow or work within it.

- The scheme doesn't reward sales people fairly and equally, so they get frustrated and either under-perform or start looking for a better job.

- One product line might be pushed while others are neglected, thereby increasing company losses.

- A poorly designed scheme might focus too much on new clients and not existing ones, leading to inequality of incentives and making it harder to earn fair commissions.

- The motivation scheme directly affects the success of the company, which in turn shows the general public the value of the company. The effectiveness of the scheme also affects company reputation in the sales industry, and if the reputation isn't good, skilled sales people won't look to the company when hunting for a new job.

Most motivation schemes have their loopholes, as it's not practical to design one that suits each salesperson equally. A company need not panic if a small minority of salespeople are deviating from the scheme, and not thriving under it. However, the sales scheme needs to be effective overall if the company is to succeed.

An Ineffective Sales Scheme Just Isn't Worth The Risk

As you can see, an ineffective motivation scheme can have several serious consequences. Sometimes these effects aren't felt at first, but may become more and more evident over time.

If there are problems with sales targets and revenues, the sales scheme is one place to look for answers. Other causes of low productivity include:

- Lack of training
- A bad product offering
- A market mismatch
- Poor positioning against the competition

The question then becomes, how can you know if the sales scheme is at fault? Let's look closer.

How To Identify Whether The Sales Scheme Is The Problem

Once it becomes clear that there's a problem somewhere in the profit margins, management need to identify whether or not the issue is related to the sales motivation scheme. Some key indicators that there is a problem with the sales scheme include:

- Payments to salespeople not being paid on time.
- Commissions that can't be accounted for.
- The number of salespeople hitting their targets is too low for the current scheme, and certainly below expectations.
- The objectives for the scheme are not being achieved.
- Salespeople are pursuing other goals which aren't the core goals for the scheme.
- Marked inequality between those performing far above the target and those performing far below the target.

All of these problems come down to one of a few core causes at the higher levels of management:

- Poor management overall
- A toxic or unhelpful company culture

- An immature product
- A poor commercial offering

My suggestion here is to go beyond the problem itself and its immediate causes, and look deeper into the underlying issues. For example, if a sales person leaves the company and you suspect it's because of the motivation scheme, that doesn't help management to improve. Rather, management must look deeper and discover which part of the motivation scheme caused the problem.

For example, we recently conducted a survey and found out that the three biggest reasons for high turnovers were:

- Wrongly set quotas
- Wrongly set tiered commissions
- An over complicated system

Simply saying "the sales scheme is the problem" isn't enough. Managers need to work out what exactly about the scheme is the problem. The best way to do that is to use analytics to see where the problems lie. Monitoring analytics means we can often identify a problem even more the serious negative consequences start. Three useful ways to do that include:

Monitoring distribution of performance. There should be a smooth distribution of performances around the hundred percent mark, with people both below and above. If eighty percent of people are making more than a hundred percent of their targets, or eighty percent are making only sixty percent of their targets, something is wrong. Awkward distribution is usually a sign of poor target allocation.

Monitoring leveraged incentives. Incentives are there to motivate sales staff to reach and exceed a hundred percent of their targets. If most of the money is being paid to sales people with rates below a hundred percent, that's a sign that the incentives rates paid below a hundred percent are too generous.

Assessing whether the top performers are also the top earners. Those who bring the biggest contribution to the company should be the ones who are making the most money.

Defining Sales Scheme Efficiency

No sales scheme is a hundred percent efficient. Every salesperson is different, with their own capabilities and skills, and every company, product, and territory is unique. No scheme can allow for every single variable and still be a hundred percent efficient.

Some people define efficiency as having the sales person make double what they did before, thus showing a large increase, and a huge turn of profits. However, this arbitrary number isn't always helpful, as there are so many variables that can affect the efficiency of a scheme.

So rather than aim for an impossible a hundred percent efficiency, I suggest defining an efficient motivation scheme as follows:

An efficient motivation scheme is one where targets are regularly exceeded, and past performances are outdone.

If a new system is implemented and it brings about a significant increase in returns, that system is a success. Improvements don't come about by themselves, and management shouldn't underestimate the seemingly miraculous difference a new motivation scheme can make.

Many managers still believe that a poorly designed system doesn't have any real impact. The truth is, a poorly designed system is a serious threat to business growth and the earlier problems can be identified and eliminated, the better.

Four Indicators Of A Problem In The Sales Scheme

In my time working in this field, I've seen the same four problems arise again and again, as an indicator that there's something wrong with a sale scheme:

1. Big Incentives Payments But Poor Results

When a company is spending a vast amount on incentives, but not seeing anything near the hoped-for result, there's a problem. This problem is widespread. In most cases the company has budgeted the amount to be spent on incentives, but not looked closely enough at how to ensure the scheme sticks to that budget. As a result, the budget is exceeded, but revenues don't rise as much as hoped.

2. Sales Targets Are Not Aligned With The Company's Objectives

Most companies set targets at the start of the year. They might be hard or soft targets, but in either case the motivation scheme needs to be in alignment with them. If the motivation scheme isn't in alignment with what the company wants to achieve, problems will quickly set in. The most common problem in this case is that the sales scheme budget has been spent down to the last penny, yet the year's targets have not been met.

3. Salespeople Leaving Shortly After Joining The Company

Salespeople need an income that covers their needs. If it's too hard to reach their targets under the current sales scheme, they'll leave, and often do so quickly. Salespeople are a significant investment for the company, so it's important to hang on to them. Not to mention that when they leave, they take with them all the skills and knowledge they gained, which competitors can then benefit from. That's not good news! Management needs to assign targets that are reachable, motivating, and exciting enough to keep salespeople striving for more, with a strong chance of success. It's also important to keep in mind that it can take up to two years for salespeople to properly settle into their role and achieve at optimum levels.

4. Success Comes At Random

Each salesperson has unique skills and abilities. The sales management put in effort to improve those skills and best fit the salesperson for their role. If the sales scheme doesn't allow for those unique abilities, management can expect to see random and unpredictable results, with some sales people lagging far behind. Consistency in both the sales scheme and in management are vital for success.

The First Step In Identifying The Problem

The first step in identifying where exactly the problem lies is to carry out a thorough analysis of the sales scheme. The earlier this can be done, the better. If management analyse the sales scheme early enough, then problems can often be headed off before they even arise, and certainly before they cause major losses to the company.

I recommend putting together a dedicated team to oversee this analysis. This team is responsible for examining the existing system, assessing its efficiency, making recommendations to improve efficiency, and making sure those recommendations are carried out.

The role of this team is not to expose the loopholes and come up with a quick fix. Rather, the role is to undertake a deep analysis and see if a change in the foundation of the scheme is needed. This information must be passed to the stakeholders so they can make an informed decision on whether or not a change in the scheme is required.

So long as it's done thoroughly, this kind of deep analysis can root out practically all problems within a sales motivation scheme.

Setting up this kind of task force is particularly important because so many companies don't realise there is a problem with their sales incentives scheme. They frequently assume the problem is coming from elsewhere in the company – quite often the sales team. For example, let's say management notices a high turnover of sales people. So many of them will point at the sales team and say "they're just not good enough!" or "they must need better training." They hardly ever look to the sales scheme itself to find the source of the problem.

Setting up a task force ensures the sales scheme is thoroughly examined and any problems identified. Now management have clear and verifiable data and information to work with, rather than randomly assigning blame.

Further Steps To Analysing The Sales Scheme

Experienced salespeople can often spot gaps and inconsistencies in the scheme even, simply by dint of their long experience. However, these seem gaps can be harder for management – who aren't in the trenches every day – to spot. That's why a full analysis benefits both salespeople and management alike, bringing all the issues out in to the open air so they can be dealt with.

Once management have agreed that a full analysis of the sales scheme is in order, it's time to map out what exactly needs to be analysed. Here are five things that any analysis must include:

1. An investigation into the cost of paying out incentives, compared to the profits made each year. This lets management see how much incentives cost balanced against monetary gains, and makes it easier to come up with a scheme that gives them full control of the cost of incentives.

2. An analysis into the rate of total incentives received by individual salespeople within a specified time frame. This lets management see if incentives payments are being evenly distributed among sales staff or not.

3. An analysis of the amount of commissions paid to a salesperson or a group of salespeople and any changes in those amounts, in the long run. This gives an overview of how sales people are performing, how new hires are doing, and whether salespeople are earning above or below target in the longer term.

4. An investigation into the overall level of performance of each sales person within a specified time period. This lets management see if the majority of salespeople are falling above or below the target line. If most are falling below, that's a clear indication that something is wrong with the system.

5. An analysis on the methods by which commissions are distributed to new versus old client accounts. This lets managers see where most commissions are being paid and whether or not that's in line with their company's aims.

The earlier a thorough analysis can be carried out, the better.

Seven Steps To Correct An Ineffective Sales Motivation Scheme

If a full analysis of the sales scheme points to a problem within it, managers will obviously be asking what to do next.

The point of a sales motivation scheme is to offer financial opportunities to salespeople, in return for their hard work. The payment of bonuses and commissions is a strong motivator for salespeople who have bills to pay, and who have a competitive nature.

There are several ways to work with an ineffective sales scheme. Managers will sometimes leap to simply capping the amount of commissions paid, but this isn't always the best way. Another popular tactic is to increase a threshold of performance to get the payment.

This scattergun approach to fixing the issue isn't effective. Before fixing the scheme, management need to remind themselves of the true purpose of any sales scheme: To increase revenues while growing their client base. Both managers and salespeople should benefit from the scheme. The managers benefit from company success, while sales people benefit from commissions earned and the chance to rise through the ranks.

With that in mind, these five steps are the best way to begin correcting an ineffective sales scheme:

- Carry out a full analysis and check whether or not the motivation scheme is helping salespeople achieve more than they were achieving previously.

- Form a competent operational committee to handle this issue going forward. This committee should include representatives from finance, HR, sales, and analytics team.

- Look at the company's plans and aims for the scheme, and make sure they dovetail with the aspirations of the sales department based on the incentives they're being offered.

- Plan the changes that need to be made in order to fix the sales scheme and bring it in line with company aims.

- Draw up a detailed plan of the steps that need to be taken, the timeframe in which they need to happen, and who is responsible for each step.

- Ensure that every department, and especially the sales team, fully understand what is going to happen, why, how it affects them, how it benefits them, and what is expected of them.

- Carry out regular and ongoing reviews of the amount of incentive being paid, how often, and how it matches up with company budgets and profits. Use these reviews to identify problems and deal with them as quickly as possible.

The sales scheme is the hinge on which company success hangs. If management notices that revenues aren't as good as they should be, or salespeople are not meeting their targets, the sales scheme is a good first place to look for answers. Thorough and ongoing analysis of the sales scheme can solve a lot of problems and prevent new ones arising in the future.

Increased Turnover Of Sales People; Why Sales People Are Leaving Your Firm And What To Do To Change That

Introduction

The world of sales can seem complicated at times, especially for busy managers who are trying to run a large sales staff and manage a complex sales motivation scheme. Figuring out how to make all the moving parts fit together into a desirable profit and continuous growth seem like an enormous task. However, when you look closer, you'll see that successful sales can be broken down into two key components: A profitable product, and a sales team. Of course, there is more to running a business than that, but if one of those two elements are missing or broken, there will be poor, or even no sales.

For any sales-based business to succeed, it needs a sellable product, and need sales staff with the skill to find prospects and make the sale.

Businesses often invest a lot of time, energy and money into their product and their sales team, which they are right to do. Successful companies understand the value of an efficient and dedicated sales force.

That's why a high turnover in the sales team is so frustrating. As any sales manager knows, building and retaining a strong team is a vital component of success. Losing sales staff is a blow to the business, especially given that it usually takes at least a year to replace a sales person and bring the new person up to full capacity.

Could The Sales Motivation Scheme Be To Blame?

When high sales team turnover is highlighted as a problem, a company naturally wants to resolve the issue as soon as possible.

The best place to start is by rooting out the cause of the high turnover so as to deal with the problem at its source. A flaw sales motivation scheme can cause high turnover, and yet it is sometimes overlooked when searching for the source of the problem.

In this report, we're going to take a look at how a flawed sales motivation scheme can lead to high turnover, how to find out if that is the root of the problem, and what steps can be taken to prevent the sales motivation scheme from causing high turnover in the future.

Why Turnover and Staff Retention Are So Important

Any employee turnover represents a time and monetary cost to a company. Here are just some of the reasons high employee turnover is a problem:

- It takes an investment of resources to find and hire the best new person for the job.

- Management may need to raise the salary for the position to get it filled quickly if the need is urgent.

- At least one staff member will need to take time out of their working day to train the new employee and get them up to the same level as the person they are replacing.

- It takes time for a new staff member to adjust to the culture of a new workplace and there is a risk that they might not fit in.

- If the new person doesn't perform as expected, more time and revenue is lost and there is a risk that the cycle will start again with more hires needed and more time and money spent finding and training them.

Any manager knows that hiring and training are resource intensive so it is better to retain staff if possible, especially highly skilled and experienced staff members.

Sales Turnover Is An Even Bigger Issue

Sales turnover is an even bigger issue than employee turnover. Why is that? Because the company is relying on its sales people for regular monthly income and therefore profits. It needs the sales team to be as effective as possible, and a new team member simply hasn't got the experience to perform as well as the rest of their teammates.

Even if they have a lot of sales experience from other companies, it still takes time to learn the ropes at the new workplace. There are many new processes and methodologies to learn, and there's no short cut for learning them. Becoming skilled at a sales role takes considerably longer than, say, an admit role.

It takes at least six months or more for a new sales person to reach maximum effectiveness and adapt to their new role and company. It takes twelve months or more for them to gain in depth understanding of the territory and the clients.

Good Sales People Are Invaluable

A good sales person has impressive skills, but their contribution is even more than that. They have a certain mentality, a drive and intelligence, and what's more, they are familiar with a company's customers. They've most likely got long term customers that they've nurtured long term relationships with. That kind of trust cannot simply be replaced if they leave. Plus, they understand and fit nicely with the company culture.

The problem gets even more complicated if a company sells a complex or technical product that requires in-depth understanding. Replacing a good sales person who understands both the product and the customers is a long and expensive task. If a company requires new hires to have a certain number of years' experience or specific skills, the pool of potential new sales people gets even smaller.

Everyone Is Affected When A Good Sales Person Leaves

If a high achieving sales person leaves the team, it has an effect on those left behind. The rest of the team needs to put in extra effort to replace the revenue and client relationships their departing colleague brought to the business.

Losing a sales person often leads to a mid-year target review for everyone else, resulting in higher targets for them.

A Stable Core Sales Force Is Good For Every Business

A stable core sales force is good for every business. Does that mean a business should never take on new sales people? Not at all. New sales people bring fresh ideas and perspectives, along with experience and even knowledge of the competition. However, as we have seen, bringing on new sales people is resource intensive, and losing good sales people causes many problems. That's why keeping a stable core sales force is a good idea:

- A core sales force that doesn't change much means that most sales people have in depth knowledge of the product, the market and the clients, all of which helps them close new deals.

- Long-term sales people often have strong client relationships, which benefit the company.

- Retaining core sales people makes it easier to forecast sales, because the company knows it can rely on its regular sales people to produce consistent results.

- Long term sales people have the insight and knowledge to spot new trends, new opportunities, and potential problems.

- Retaining a core sales team directly impacts profit. A strong core team with occasional new people provides a perfect balance of reliability and some new ideas.

Keeping hold of the best sales people is a pressing concern for any company. Let's turn our attention to an important cause of high turnover: A flawed sales motivation scheme.

How A Flawed Sales Motivation Scheme Causes High Turnover

A flawed sales motivation scheme is one of the main reasons for high turnover of sales people.

A Sales Motivation Scheme Sets Expectations

When a sales person is hired, there is an agreement that he will receive a certain amount of pay for what he does. This often has a fixed part and a commission-based element, although schemes do of course vary.

If the sales person is told to expect excellent opportunities to earn commissions, and those opportunities don't materialize, they will feel cheated and unmotivated. Most likely they will start looking for a job that offers better earning potential.

For example, if a sales motivation scheme offers fifteen percent of new revenues to a sales person, but they need to bring eighty percent of their quota before getting a payout, the chances of actually making those earnings are significantly decreased. Now the sales person feels disgruntled and decides decent earnings are far out of his grasp, so he starts looking for another job where it is easier to earn money.

Is A Changing Sales Motivation Scheme The Problem?

Another way a flawed motivation scheme affects turnover is when the scheme changes in a way that makes life harder for the sales team. For example, if the scheme changes so that:

- Sales staff now get paid less despite putting in the same effort as before.
- There are ostensibly chances to earn more, but the extra effort needed to do so is immense.
- Payments seem to be split more unevenly between staff that were involved in landing a deal, so some staff members are getting less than their fair share.
- Frequent changes make it hard to keep up with what is expected, and what level of commissions will be paid.

In cases like this, the sales people involved will most likely feel the scheme has become unfair. This leads to poor staff morale and contributes to higher staff turnover.

Disputes and Bad Communication Contribute To High Turnover

If staff frequently find themselves caught in disputes about payments, they will grow disgruntled with the current sales scheme.

Staff need to know that if they put in the effort, they will be fairly rewarded, with no disputes or miscommunication. If staff constantly need to contact management or HR to get something sorted out before they can get paid, there's a problem.

Sometimes The Sales Policy Is The Problem

Say for example a sales person brings a very large sale that isn't covered by the existing sales policy. Management don't want to make a payout of that size that they hadn't budgeted for, but naturally the sales person wants to be paid for their effort and for winning such a lucrative contract.

A sales policy needs to cover all eventualities, to avoid such situations arising.

The sales policy also needs to be a little flexible. For example, if more than one sales person works together to win a sale, the scheme must allow for them both to be compensated. Nor should it be so strict that the team ends up penalized over missing one single prerequisite for payment.

Is The Grass Greener?

If sales staff find that a competitor offers a much better sales scheme, or that their current employer's commissions are below the usual rate for their market, there's a good chance they'll look for a job with better pay and conditions.

A company who wants to keep its sales staff needs to know what the competition is offering, and make sure that they meet or exceed that in terms of commission scheme, benefits, and company culture.

A good sales scheme is one that offers staff the potential to earn good money, and to find and nurture new sales opportunities. It's up to management to make sure staff have enough opportunities to earn commissions, and a fair motivation scheme that supports and motivates them in meeting their targets and earning commissions.

How To Tell If The Sales Motivation Scheme Is Behind High Turnover

Some turnover is to be expected in any organisation. However, if high turnover is becoming an issue and the company suspects the sales motivation scheme is to blame, it's time to investigate whether the scheme is be the source of the problem.

Who Is Leaving?

Some amount of turnover is normal, especially if those leaving are low performers or people who don't really click with the team and culture. However, if numbers are high or rising and top earners are leaving, that's a clear sign something is wrong.

If turnover is obviously too high, it's time to start tracking who leaves and analysing the information. Management should keep track of:

- Who leaves
- The key points raised during the exit interview
- What their performance was like over the last three years
- Which territory they were covering
- What targets they were set
- How often they met targets
- What commissions they were earning

Regular Interviews Help Pinpoint Sales Motivation Issues

Regular interviews with sales staff and sales managers are helpful for pinpointing issues with the sales motivation scheme.

The people who are using the scheme are the ones who are best placed to talk about what works, and point out what doesn't.

Once or twice-yearly interviews are a good tool for assessing the ongoing success (or not) of the scheme. It's also a good idea to carry out interviews if the system is changed, or a new system is introduced.

Collect And Analyse The Right Data

As well as interviews and assessing staff turnover, there are several other metrics that can help a company ascertain whether their sales motivation scheme is a problem:

- Performance analytics. How is each person performing? How does that compare to the rest of the team and to their own performance history?

- Historical payments by each team member. Look for big deviations between staff members, or in each individual's performance record. If there is a change, check whether a change in the scheme took place at the same time.

- Territory and target allocation. Analyse the historic performance in each territory, and use the information to predict future prospects for that region and any potential difficulties such as maturity or competition.

- Activities that are not direct selling. Are sales people helping with product development, or offering support with marketing objectives, for example? And if they are, are they being fairly compensated for activities that don't directly generate commissions?

- The distribution of performance and payments. For example, if only five percent of the sales force is meeting nearly a hundred percent of their target, but the rest are only meeting sixty percent of their targets, there is a problem.

- Performance by territory. How is each territory performing compared to other territories and to its own history?

Thorough, ongoing analysis and regular communication are key to ensuring the sales motivation scheme is not a problem.

The Top Three Sales Motivation Scheme Elements That Can Lead To High Staff Turnover

Once an organisation realises that the sales motivation scheme is flawed, it's time to dig into the program itself and find out what, specifically, is causing issues.

The easiest way to do this is by honing in on the different components of the sales scheme, one at a time, in order to isolate the issue.

There are three main areas that are top suspects when it comes to causing problems:

1. Territory

Territory assignment can cause a lot of stress to the sales force if it's not well designed. For example, if one sales person is making huge commissions in an established and easy territory, while another is struggling to penetrate a new and not very lucrative territory, they might get frustrated and leave.

Territory isn't just about the geographical area. It also covers factors such as the size of the accounts, or the specific products that are being sold, or industries that are being sold to.

No matter how territories are allocated, all sales people should, as much as possible, have equal opportunities to land new clients, make commissions, and earn similar money to their clients.

2. Quota

Quota size has the potential to frustrate sales people can cause a lot of conflicts, especially if the quotas are uneven across the sales force. Trying to reach a target of $500,000 is far different to trying to reach $2,000,000. Even smaller differences matter.

Sales quotas must correspond to the ability of the territory to produce enough sales and leads to meet that quota.

Of course, quotas should be challenging, or the motivation scheme won't work, but there must be around a seventy percent chance of the sales person meeting their target if they work reasonably hard.

Unattainable sales targets are a quick way to frustrate sales people and prompt them to look for a better job.

3. Incentive Scheme Mechanics

Incentive scheme mechanics covers all the moving parts that make the scheme fit together: Terms and conditions, the pay mix, the leverage that the program pays, multipliers, incentive caps and so on.

The design of the incentive scheme is key. One small flaw can derail the whole program. For example, what is the leverage if a sales person sells more than a hundred percent of their target? If they're not well compensated for such outstanding performance, they might well go elsewhere.

It's better to go over every element and every potential situation with a fine-tooth comb now, than to find out later that a small flaw is causing a ripple effect and more and more staff are leaving.

Take Steps To Prevent Problems Before They Arise

Often by the time a flaw in the sales motivation scheme is flagged up, it's too late to respond adequately. The longer a problem goes unresolved, the worse the consequences are likely to be.

Instead, companies need to analyse their sales scheme regularly and put a process in place to identify potential problems before they grow.

Taking the following steps will help any organisation establish a process that flags problems early:

- In every exit interview, ask the departing sales person if the motivation scheme was part of their decision to leave, and if so, what specifically about it did they dislike.
- In every induction, ask the new person how much importance the motivation scheme played in their decision to join.
- Regularly assess all the data listed in earlier in this report.
- Look at targets met in the last year. Look to about seventy percent of the sales force meeting their targets, with no more than twenty percent making between fifty and a hundred percent and no more than ten percent falling below fifty percent of their targets.
- Make sure the sales motivation scheme is designed to pay well based on the above principle.
- Make sure good performances are rewarded with generosity and solving a difficult problem is met with appropriate remuneration.

- Assess the full cost of hiring and training a new sales person. Remember to include everything from the cost of advertising the position and hiring the new person, to training them and providing any equipment they need. Also remember to include any potential lost sales while the new person is brought up to speed. Seeing in black and white how much it costs to replace a sales person is a strong incentive for taking steps to boost retention.

Complementary Areas To Assess

Although we are chiefly looking at sales motivation scheme problems, there are some peripheral areas that directly impact performance, so it's a good idea to look at those, too:

Product – if the product is weak, no sales motivation scheme can compensate. Make sure the project is well positioned and competitive.

Sales support – sales people need attention and support of managers, and help with identifying initiatives and executing a sales plan.

Administrative support – sales people can lose precious time in approvals, legal documents, operational entries and other admin. The sales force needs administrative support so they lose less time on admin and have more time to dedicate to selling.

Start Assessing Now

As we've seen, the consequences of high turnover are serious both in terms of cost, amount of sales made, and staff morale. That's why developing the right processes and continuously evaluating the sales motivation scheme should be priorities.

One way of keeping abreast of issues is to set up a team or assign someone within an existing team who is responsible for tracking all the data and keeping an eye on all the potential red flags that are laid out in this document.

Split responsibility between HR, sales, and finance. Ask HR teams to track turnover and note down the results of exit interviews and inductions. Ask finance to keep watch on the cost of commissions and track the ratio between the profit margin of the product and the cost of its commissions. Finally, ask sales to monitor the satisfaction of the sales force and their performance.

Establish policies and workflows for every aspect of the sales motivation scheme. This ensures that the calculation and payment of incentives and the operation of the scheme is smooth. Make sure the policy document includes all different areas of the incentive scheme so that there are less delays, less hiccups, and less unexpected happenings.

Sales Roles, Their Responsibilities And Eligibility For Sales Incentives. Why Defining The Sales Roles Is The First Thing To Consider

The sales incentive scheme is key to the success of any company that relies on selling products or services. After all, the sales incentive scheme determines how much sales people stand to earn. The most effective sales incentive scheme is one that truly motivates sales staff to reach or exceed targets (depending on company aims) and keeps them engaged with their roles.

Common Errors To Avoid When Designing A Sales Motivation Scheme

Designing a sales scheme is no easy task. To do so well requires knowledge, skills, and discipline. Not to mention the willingness to evaluate and re-evaluate over and over until it's working exactly as it should work.

There are some common errors that I've seen show up again and again when helping companies design their sales schemes. Being aware of these will help you avoid the same pitfalls:

Not knowing who has a sales role

It's easy to assume that only sales people who are out there direct selling to clients have a sales role. However, there are lots of other roles that contribute to successful sales, such as technical support.

Not defining sales roles clearly enough

Staff and management need to be clear on the responsibilities of each sales role, and know exactly how that role adds value to the organisation.

Not understanding who is involved in each sales role

Sometimes people from other teams or departments are involved in a successful sale, and it's important that those people not be overlooked.

Not defining which products are to be sold

Sometimes the sales role itself is perfectly clear in terms of responsibilities and who performs the role – but there's still a grey area when it comes to what the sales person is actually responsible for selling!

Outdated motivation schemes

I've seen plenty of companies make the mistake of changing a sales role and its responsibilities, but neglecting to update the sales motivation scheme to match.

Piling on too many additional responsibilities

If a sales person has too many additional responsibilities that aren't part of the compensation scheme, it prevents them giving as much focus as they should to their sales role. This is frustrating for managers and salespeople alike.

Not providing enough resources and support

Sometimes traditional direct selling to the client just doesn't cut it and a salesperson needs to seek out internal collaboration or external partnerships. If they don't have the necessary support and resources in place, it will directly affect their performance.

All these mistakes can create weaknesses in a sales motivation scheme. However, if I were to sum it up in one sentence it would be this: An ill-defined sales role is one of the biggest threats to the success of a sales motivation scheme.

The Sales Role Is Central To Any Incentive Program

The purpose of any compensation scheme is to motivate the sales force, and each person within it.

It's important to remember that the design of the sales scheme is about incentivizing sales roles rather than individual sales people. What do I mean by this? Think of it this way: Although there are times that one sales person gets different commission rates than another in an equivalent role, it's rare. In most cases the level of compensation for each role isn't based on the person performing it, but on the role itself.

Imagine a company that sells telecommunication products across the U.S. They might have one group of salespeople that focus on selling a specific flagship product. Meantime, another group of sales people is tasked with managing accounts and retaining existing relationships rather than making new ones. The first group is all about selling to new clients, while the second is far more concerned with cross selling and upselling to existing clients.

In this case, the sales compensation scheme shouldn't be designed around the individual people in each role, but around the roles themselves. All of those in the first group should be treated equally when it comes to compensation and incentives. Likewise, all those in the second group should have the same opportunities when it comes to reaching their targets.

Sales people performing identical sales roles should always share the same objectives, and have similar targets, financial opportunities, and opportunities to reach their targets.

Designing the scheme around each type of role in this way creates a fair work environment. So, where should management start?

Creating Well Defined Sales Roles

If sales incentives schemes are built around sales roles, then it's important to make sure those sales roles are well defined.

A lack of well-defined sales roles creates confusion for management and staff alike, and risks decreasing the efficiency of the sales compensation scheme.

A well-defined sales role is one in which both the sales person and the management understand:

- The responsibilities of the role
- The sales person's objectives and targets
- Which activities the sales person is expected to carry out
- How the sales person's performance is measured

However, for a sales scheme to be truly effective, managers need to go a step further and decide exactly which part of the sales role should be incentivized. Which part of the role will be rewarded via the sales compensation scheme? For example:

- The sales person's ability to identify and woo potential clients

- Managing the installation of a tech solution that the company is selling
- Signing new clients
- Increasing upsells to existing clients

The list goes on and on, depending on the objectives of the company. In most cases, the most important part of any role is the ability to persuade a potential client to think differently about their situation, and thus to get them excited to buy the product or service. However, just because this seems obvious, that doesn't mean management should skip this step or make assumptions. A clearly defined sales role and an assessment of which parts are incentivized makes for a much more effective sales compensation scheme.

The Consequences Of Not Defining The Sales Role Clearly Enough

A failure to properly define a sales role has a multitude of effects which can ultimately affect the success of a company.

Confusion

Not defining a role leads to confusion among not only the sales force itself, but also stakeholders, management, and the incentives design team. After all, how can you design an incentives scheme if you don't understand clearly what the sales force is supposed to achieve?

Paying sales people for the wrong reasons

If the sales role isn't properly defined, management don't know exactly which part of the role is supposed to be incentivized. As we talked about above, is it direct sales? Keeping existing clients? Finding new leads? For example, if an account manager is responsible for upselling to existing clients, but the commission scheme doesn't actually incentivize him for doing so, confusion reigns. And the manager won't be very motivated.

Missing key targets

If sales people don't have well defined roles or properly understand what it is they're being motivated to do, it's much harder for them to hit their targets.

High turnover in the sales department

When sales roles are poorly defined, it's difficult for sales people to understand, reach, and exceed their targets. That means less commissions for them, poor job satisfaction, and ultimately a move to a company that gives them a better chance of making good money.

How To Evaluate A Sales Role

To start with, look at the big picture. For each sales role, ask where it fits in terms of the clients worked with. For example:

- New business roles that focus on acquiring new clients.
- Account managers that focus on existing relationships.
- Key account managers that focus on the most important clients.

Once you have a general picture of the sales role, you need to understand how many different sales channels each role has access to. Who do they sell to? Do they sell to end clients, or to an intermediary?

There are many ways to "group" sales roles. Here are some of the ways of grouping sales roles, that I've seen my own clients use:

- Account managers
- New sales
- Business development
- Overlay sales
- Sales specialists
- Key/strategic/major account managers
- By customer target
- New accounts
- Existing accounts
- Channel partners
- Channel end-users
- By customer segment

- Big/Small account
- Stratified customer
- Product/application
- Industry sales
- Geographic (sales territory) sales

Now you have your sales roles generally grouped, it's time to get into the finer details of each sales role. For each role, ask:

What is the sales person's involvement in running sales opportunities?

What specific responsibilities does each sales person have? Identify their level of involvement in:

- Identifying potential customers
- Qualifying potential customers
- Proposing solutions and giving demonstrations
- Commercials
- Closing the sale
- Fulfilling the commitment

What is the sales person's relationship to the clients?

Consider how and when they participate in the sales process. Identify their level of involvement in:

- Creating demand for the product or service
- Educating customers about the product or services
- Buyer identification and / or qualification
- Nurturing relationships
- Purchase commitment
- Fulfilling and / or delivering orders
- After sales service

What additional factors need consideration?

Some other factors worth considering include:

- How the sales role fits within the team. Many sales are the result of effort from several people.
- How hard the product is to sell. How well would it sell through marketing alone, without a sales person involved?
- What other tasks does the salesperson have to carry out? Marketing and administrative tasks, for example, might take away from time spent direct selling, but are still a vital part of the role.
- What is the purpose of the sales role? Is it just to sell and bring revenue, or is it to create interest in the product and influence the state of the market?

Is Sales Role Eligible For Compensation?

Now each role is defined and grouped, it's time to decide whether each role is eligible for sales incentives.

This seems obvious. If a salesperson sells a product, they deserve an incentive, right? That's true – no salesperson will sell for you if they don't have an incentive to do so!

But many companies overlook roles that aren't directly involved in selling, but are still sales roles nonetheless.

For example, I once worked with a technology company that sold a complicated product. Because of the level of complexity, they employed pre-sales consultants who regularly met with the sales manager to strategize for the business. Although they didn't have sales targets, their role was key in generating opportunities. We agreed to make the consultants eligible for sales incentives, and within a year they'd increased sales by twenty three percent.

Here are some other examples to think about:

A mature product that sells largely on the strength of its marketing team. This might include campaigns and lead generation via a website, email campaigns, or social media, which in turn creates demand and delivers qualified leads to the sales team.

The company has a strong marketing and inside sales team that does an excellent job of identifying buyer personas, and approaching people in such a way as to turn them from leads into prospects. This work saves sales people a lot of time.

Sales are made in part due to the support of sales consultants or other support staff.

Sales people work alongside a pre-sales technical support team, whose answers to technical questions play a significant part in eventually closing a deal.

The one thing you must consider when deciding on the eligibility of a sales role for compensation

The one thing you must consider when deciding on the eligibility of a sales role is the relationship with the customer.

Look at it this way: A sales role is one that involves a significant relationship with the customer, and drives that relationship towards specific milestones. A sales role requires significant contact and engagement with prospects and customers, with a view to persuading them to take action.

A sales role must also be defined by clear and quantifiable sales objectives, which can be reached by way of the client relationship.

Other things to consider for each sales role

When defining a sales role, you need to go beyond direct sales, and consider the following:

Who sets the targets?

Sales people don't set their own targets. Just as in the example I gave of the technology company, it's up to management to decide on the sales targets for each eligible role.

What is the lead generation process like?

Lead generation takes a lot of work. For some sales roles, there's a whole team that brings qualified leads, so the sales person's sole responsibility is to run the opportunity to closure. In other cases, the salesperson must hunt for leads. When defining a sales role, it's vital to look at the entire end to end process the role entails.

Who decides the sales strategy?

Who decides on the go-to sales strategy, and communicates it to the sales people?

What is the life cycle of a sale?

Taking an opportunity from lead generation to closure can be a long process. It might involve work with the stakeholders of a company. It frequently involves legal work, and don't forget the technical stage of implementing your product or solution if necessary.

A salesperson could be responsible for all or some of these tasks, and some of them take time away from direct selling.

What support does the sales role get?

Sales roles might get support from managers, marketers, administrators, or others. When defining the role, it helps to know who supports that role, and how that support contributes to the main sales role.

The Next Steps

By now it's clear that identifying which sales roles are eligible for incentives is not straightforward. However, it's worthy work that if done right can greatly enhance your company's success and the job satisfaction of your sales staff.

Start with what I call the pre-design phase. These are the things that must be done to lay the foundation before you design a sales compensation scheme. Start with these four steps:

- First, identify all the different sales roles and clearly set out the responsibilities of each.

- Now, analyse how each role works in terms of building relationships and persuading customers to action.

- Create a spreadsheet or list. For each role, note down job responsibilities, the relationship to the customer, and where the role is positioned in terms of each sales opportunity.
- Finally, decide for each role whether it's eligible for compensation as a sales role.

Sales is much more complex than it first seems. By properly identifying which roles in your company count as sales roles, you can build an effective sales compensation scheme that motivates each person to carry out their part to the best of their abilities and beyond.

Target Cash Compensation, Pay Mix And Leverage; The First Technical Terms Of The System. Defining The Total Compensation For A Sales Role, Decide How To Split Into A Fixed And A Variable Part And How One Would Pay For Excellent Performance

Any organisation that relies on a sales force needs an effective sales incentive scheme to encourage their team to optimum performance. Total target cash compensation (known as TTCC henceforth) is one of the biggest factors to decide. Let's take a closer look at how best to do that.

TTCC Is The Foundation Of A Sales Incentive Scheme

Imagine you meet a sales person in the street. This sales person also happens to be a very good friend, so they're quite happy to share their salary with you. How much would you expect a sales person to tell you they were earning? $40,000 a year? $60,000? $100,000?

When you imagine that figure, do you think your friend is referring to their fixed salary only, or to their fixed salary plus commissions?

Now imagine you're listening in on a discussion between a recruiter and a would-be sales person. There's a high chance the recruiter will talk about the total package including commissions, not just the fixed salary.

So in general, a sales person's salary is their fixed salary plus their incentives. Look at any sales contract and you'll find that sales incentives are included in the contractual terms (or if they're not, they really should be!) The incentives, or variable part of the salary, might fluctuate massively from zero to a large uncapped amount, depending on how the system was designed.

However, the variable part is never an unknown. The variable part represents the sales person's total salary if they meet or exceed every one of their targets.

Having a thorough understanding of both the fixed and variable part of the sales compensation scheme is a must for sales managers, and the foundation of an effective incentive scheme.

Why Is TTCC So Important?

Sales management needs to know how much money a salesperson will get paid if they reach a hundred percent of their targets. This is vital for sales budgeting and employee payroll, which is one of the biggest operating expenses in any company.

TTCC is also key to both recruitment and managing the existing team. The TTCC figure lets a sales person know what they can expect to earn if they reach their targets. It lets them know what manner of financial reward to expect for a job well done.

When deciding on the TTCC, it's important to remember that it's linked to a specific sales role, not to an individual person. Naturally the TTCC might vary a bit depending on a sales person's experience or seniority, but the TTCC is still attached to a role and not a person. Managers should keep this in mind and make sure the TTCC they decide on is suited to the specific role it's attached to, even if a different person takes on that role.

Surveys and research into the current market and what competitors pay for similar roles can also help managers decide.

Four Approaches To Setting The TTCC Level

There are four main ways to decide on the total cash compensation for a sales role.

1. Competition

Most companies today use the competition approach. They gather information on what the market is generally paying for similar roles. They might employ a consulting firm to do research on their behalf.

2. Profit margin

Another approach is to use the products profit margin. Managers start by deciding on a percentage of the profit margin to be used as an incentive. This incentive is built in to the variable part of the TTCC. Next, they decide on the fixed salary by deciding how much they want to pay on top of the variable amount.

3. Revenue sharing

Companies can also take a revenue sharing approach. In this model, the company gives sales people a certain percentage of overall revenue, regardless of the profitability of doing so.

4. Total cost

Finally, companies can take a total cost approach. They decide at the beginning of the year what their total budget is for incentives for that year. For example, a company might decide it wants to allocate $5 million for incentives that year. This budget can then be split between sales people based on their targets.

Important Factors To Consider When Deciding TTCC

There are several factors that affect the final TTCC decision. It's important that managers keep all of them in mind, to ensure the TTCC figure they reach is the one that will best serve their objectives, and motivate their team.

Here are some factors that need consideration:

Company objectives

The company's objectives are one of the biggest deciding factors. What are they trying to achieve? What are their current challenges? What are their objectives in terms of their sales force? Are they focused on building a good relationship with their employees? Are they looking to reduce turnover, attract the right sales people, increase loyalty, or all three?

Company status

What is the company's current market share? How strong is their reputation? Are they well established enough to make sales based on their name alone, or do they have a way to go? Is it a startup or a mature business?

The state of the industry

How competitive is the industry? Is the company well known within it, or are they relatively new? A start up trying to gain market share will need a different TTCC than a well-established company, and will likely have a very different budget.

The sales role

Which sales role is the TTCC attached to, and how challenging is it? Could a new salesperson do it, or does it require an experienced hand? How complex is the role? How much value can the right salesperson in that role create of the client, and more importantly, how much scope is there for them to guide the client into a buying decision?

The sales role is a big deciding factor in whether to opt for a higher TTCC. If a sales role ticks any of the boxes below, a higher TTCC could be appropriate:

- It's a highly skilled role where the sales person needs a thorough understanding of the market and competitive landscape.
- The role stretches beyond sales into business development activities such as seeking out new business and forging new relationships.
- The sales person has a significant relationship with the customer and a strong ability to influence their buying decisions.
- The market is a difficult one to sell to.
- The market is such that effective sales people are hard to come by.

A lower TTCC is appropriate if:

- The sales person doesn't need exceptional knowledge.
- Softer sales skills are enough.
- The customer has various touch points in the company along their journey to buying, thus the salesperson is just one of many.
- The market is saturated with candidates who could carry out the role effectively.

Should You Pay At, Below Or Above The Market Level?

Often when a company realises there's a problem such as low production or high turnover of sales people, they jump straight to changing the sales incentives scheme. However, this isn't the only potential cause, and management needs to look at issues such as the sales team's knowledge of their product, or the need for a better promotional process for sales people.

Sometimes the problem is with interpretation and communication of the sales scheme, rather than with the sales scheme itself.

However, once a company has determined that the problem really is the sales scheme, TTCC is a good place to start looking for solutions.

For many sales managers, one of the key dilemmas is whether to pay the market rates, or go above or below. It's easier than ever to find out what the competition is paying their sales people – but the question is where to pitch your own pay level by comparison.

To answer this dilemma, a company must think about both short and long term plans and goals.

Paying the market rate

Most companies opt with paying what the competition pays, and this is a perfectly fair choice. It keeps you competitive with others in your field.

Pros: Puts you in line with the competition. Doesn't carry the risks of paying either above or below the market rate.

Cons: Your company doesn't stand out as offering particularly good incentives (if that's an area in which you wish to stand out.) Some start ups might struggle to pay market rates.

Paying above the market rate

If your company's main objective is to build revenues quickly, and the product justifies this aim, paying above the market rate is a way to attract sales people.

Pros: Can quickly attract skilled sales people who are looking to make money fast. Higher incentives can lead to more sales.

Cons: Difficult to build long lasting relationships with staff and clients alike due to the risk of higher sales staff turnovers.

Paying below the market rate

There are times when a company chooses to pay below the market rate, often for budgetary reasons. In these cases, it's a good idea to offset the lower pay with other incentives, such as a reduced risk of losing one's job.

Pros: Keeps the sales payment budget lower. In some cases, sales staff become more attached to the overall job satisfaction and become loyal to the company as a result.

Cons: Risk of losing staff to higher paying competitors. Harder to stand out from other companies unless your other benefits far outshine the lower wages.

The decision on how much to pay is one of the most important choices to make before designing a sales motivation scheme. If a company needs to sell products or services, then it needs a stable and productive sales team. The decision on how much to pay should always be made based on which payment level best serves the company's long-term goals and the creation of a strong sales force.

Managers should keep in mind the culture and principles of the company as a whole, as well as long and short term objectives.

The Next Step – Deciding On The Pay Mix

So, now your company knows how much it wants to pay in total target cash compensation for a sales role. The next step is deciding how to split it between the fixed and variable parts of the salary. For example, should the fixed part by greater than the variable, and why? Will this always be the case or will it change under different scenarios?

The split between fixed and variable pay has a direct impact on the motivation and job satisfaction of a sales person.

For example, let's say Robin has just joined your company. This is a new sales role as you're trying to build a new market and expand to new geographical regions. Management has decided to pay fifty percent fixed and fifty percent variable salary. The average sales cycle for this product, especially in new territories, is two years.

Give it a year and Robin will have handed in their resignation and signed up for a competitor. Why? Because it's taken them six months to find a lead and qualify it to an opportunity, and they've already figured out it's going to take another two years to run the opportunity through to closure. That's only fifty percent of the total possible pay for nearly three years before Robin can start earning that other fifty percent variable portion. No wonder they jumped ship!

This example illustrates why the pay mix is such an important decision.

Main Factors To Consider When Deciding The Pay Mix

Where should a company begin when deciding on the pay mix? Based on my experience, there are certain factors that should steer management more towards one option or the other.

When To Put More Weight On The Fixed Salary

There are several situations where it's more effective to put weight on the fixed salary:

- When the role has a heavy emphasis on client relationships and less on sales numbers, put more weight on the fixed salary. An example of this is account managers.

- When there's a lot of team work involved in closing the sale, especially when success is measured in the longer term.

- When other factors, such as brand awareness and marketing, play a significant role in sales, so it's not all down to the effort of one salesperson.

- When the company already has a good market share and reputation, and their objective is to retain existing customers rather than look for new ones.

- When the product is a complex one that already has good penetration in the market.

- When the sales process and cycle are complex and unpredictable.

- When the role includes lots of activities besides pure selling.

When To Put More Weight On The Variable Salary

There are also a few situations where it's more effective to put more weight on the variable part of the salary:

- The sales person has a high level of influence over whether a customer buys.
- The chances of closing a sale are high, and mostly predictable.
- The role gives a sales person control over the entire sales cycle and gives them a hand in its ultimate destiny.
- The landscape is a competitive one and every single sale matters.

As you can see, the decision on how to balance the payment mix is based on several factors. The characteristics of the sales role, the available sales opportunities, the customers, the target audience, the company's reputation and recognition, market engagement, customer awareness, and even the culture of the company, all play a part in the decision.

Assess The Mix Frequently

Once a company decides on the right fixed / variable mix, it's important not to get complacent. Managers should assess the mix frequently and make sure it's still appropriate for the job at hand.

There are certain warning signs that alert a company to the fact that the mix is wrong.

If the company notices that the expense of the salaries isn't proportionate to the sales that are coming in, then the fixed part is too high. Also be on the lookout for sales people not being motivated to bring in extra revenue, or not showing any urgency to bring in business and get deals closed.

If sales people seem to be paid excessive amounts compared to other employees and the company is starting to lose track of its longer-term objectives because salespeople are all about the big sales right now, the variable aspect is too big.

Other warning signs include customer complaints that the sales tactics are too pressured, and after sales support is poor.

The incentives scheme is one of the most important tools in a company's toolbox. It's what motivates the sales team to reach their goals and perform at their best. That's why it's important to keep checking the mix, making sure it's right, and adjusting as needed.

Leverage – The Reward For Exceeding Sales Targets

So far, we've discussed how to structure TTCC in terms of fixed and variable parts of the salary. However, there is one more aspect we need to discuss – leverage. Leverage means the potential (and often high) earnings paid to sales people who perform beyond their targets. Leverage refers to the amount a salesperson can be paid on top of both the fixed and variable part of their salary, if they perform exceptionally.

In short, leverage is the amount a company is willing to pay its very best performers (typically the top five to ten percent of sales people in the whole company.)

Leverage is often expressed as 2x or 3x, or 1:1 or 2:1. For example, if a sales person is on a scheme with a top target of $40,000 that pays 2x leverage, then the leverage is an additional $40,000. The total payout is then $80,000 or 2x the original amount.

Before deciding on leverage amounts, the sales managers must ask themselves two questions:

- Do they want to give top earners the potential to make large amounts of money on top of their existing salary?
- Do they want to make their top sales earners an example to the rest of the team of what is possible for high achievers?

Leverage is more of a psychological tool than a financial one. If the scheme is set up correctly the leverage payments should only go to the top five to ten percent of the sales force, and so shouldn't cost the company a huge amount of money. However, the leverage payments are a strong motivating force, both for the top earners who have a genuine chance of hitting those targets, and for the rest of the team who can see how much they'll earn if they reach the top tier.

Why Include Leverage In A Sales Compensation Scheme?

Some companies might feel that even if leverage is only paid to the top five to ten percent of their team, it's still an extra financial burden. However, it's a burden that's absolutely worth it, for three reasons:

- Some sales people simply do not meet their targets. As a result, top performers end up picking up the slack. Leverage rewards those top earners and recognises their extra effort and contribution.

- Leverage sets high expectations for sales people and encourages them to aim high. If a scheme has no leverage for those hitting over a hundred percent of targets, most people won't try to reach that a hundred percent and will plateau out at about ninety percent. If sales people know they'll be rewarded for reaching 120 percent of their target, they'll aim for that, and more of them will hit the hundred percent mark.

- Seeing where you could go is far more motivating than seeing where you already are! Leverage shows sales people that they have the potential to go much further.

Let's look at another practical example. If a sales scheme pays seven percent compensation for up to a hundred percent of the sales target, but pays fifteen percent for anything over a hundred percent, that lets staff know that over-performance will be handsomely rewarded. Now they have a compelling reason to keep bringing in sales even after reaching a hundred percent of their target.

In my years in the field I've found that the most effective incentives schemes are the ones that encourage staff to not only meet their goals, but to stretch beyond them.

Does Your Company Need A Leverage Scheme?

Not every company has a leverage scheme. I recommend that any company who doesn't, makes a firm decision on whether to introduce one. That way, they know what happens when someone reaches a hundred percent of the target, and can communicate that to the sales force.

Deciding whether to have a leverage scheme comes down to one simple question:

When sales people reach their targets, do you want them to stop selling, or do you want them to keep selling?

If you want them to keep selling, you need leverage to encourage them to do that. Building leverage into your rewards scheme is the easiest and fairest way to reward high earners. That way, everyone (including management) knows exactly what to expect.

Let's look at an example.

If a salesperson is reaching sixty percent of their sales targets, then the sales incentive scheme motivates them to reach a hundred percent. But what happens when they reach that hundred percent? Leverage motivates them to reach 120 percent.

Some sale schemes are designed so that earning over a hundred percent of the target is not possible. However, many companies find that the best thing is to build in payments for those who perform over target. That's where leverage comes in.

Downsides Of Paying Leverage – And What To Do About Them

It's clear that leverage is a powerful motivator for any sales team. However, as with anything in business, there are positives and negatives to consider. Keeping the downsides in mind means you can plan your scheme carefully and mitigate risk as much as possible.

Here are three main drawbacks to paying leverage – and what you can do about them.

- If the scheme isn't planned carefully, your company could end up paying huge sums in leverage payments.

What to do: Be careful when assigning targets. If the targets are too easy to reach, more people will exceed them, and you'll need to pay more leverage. Set them so that only the top sales people can exceed them.

- Having a negative effect on staff motivation. Leverage is supposed to motivate staff. However, if the salary for those who don't exceed their targets is too low, staff will get fed up and stop trying. If the only way to get a decent paycheck is to be one of the few that exceeds targets, that's not motivating.

What to do: Make sure your sales compensation scheme offers fair remuneration for all staff who reach a hundred percent or near a hundred percent of their targets, not just the overachievers.

- Sales people trying to game the system. For example, a salesperson might delay closing a sale until the next sales period if they realise they're not in a position to get a leverage payment, because they hope pushing the sale forward to the next period will help them get a payment next time.

What to do: Be mindful of the risk of manipulation when designing or tweaking the system. Keep tabs on sales records so you can spot any patterns that show sales people saving up sales in order to win leverage.

I believe leverage is a vital part of any sales compensation scheme. It lets your sales staff know that extra effort is recognised, valued and compensated – and the psychological power of that cannot be underestimated. The key is careful scheme design so that only the top five to ten percent can achieve leverage, but those who do not still get good compensation for their work.

Calculating Leverage

Broadly speaking, there are three ways to pay leverage:

- Pay the same as others in the industry.

- Choose your figures based on making an example for others to follow – how much does leverage need to be to motivate the sales team to aim high?
- Decide based on what is most affordable while still encouraging sales people to over perform.

In addition, I recommend considering the following when calculating leverage:

What is considered top performer status?

How do you define a top performer (typically around five to ten percent of the sales force)? How many people does management want in that group?

How much are management willing to pay?

Be very clear on how much the company wants to reward a top performer as compared to those who reach at or just below a hundred percent of their targets.

Will there be a cap?

Putting an earning cap in place or decelerating payouts once a certain level is reached can help keep leverage payments manageable. Of course, for some teams no cap is necessary and unlimited earning potential is part of the draw of the role.

Where does this fit with company culture?

What has management's approach been so far when it comes to motivating staff to over achieve? How does big payments to over achievers fit with this? How do management want to promote high leverage roles?

What stage of development is the company at?

Newer companies with less established reputations often need to provide extra motivation to sales staff in order to get an early boost on sales and start building their market.

What does the high leverage role look like?

For example, if the role is quite low earning and has some challenges, then a high leverage payment is a good way to motivate salespeople to work hard.

How was last year's performance?

Take a look at the figures for each sales person. What kind of effort does a sales person need to make in order to get over a hundred percent of their target? How many people are doing that already (this will affect how much leverage needs to be paid)? Is it always the same people that overachieve targets?

Getting the pay mix right is vital to the success of the total target cash compensation scheme. The balance between fixed, variable, and leverage payments determines how motivated sales people are, and thus whether or not they achieve their company's goals.

Different Designs For A Company To Choose From – From Bonus To Commission Schemes, Pool Bonus And Team Incentives, Why All These Fit Different Business Models

Introduction

It's not easy to decide on a sales incentives scheme. There is so much to decide: Commissions, bonuses, flat payments, points system and more.

Even once you decide how much to pay your sales team, there are still questions to answer. What triggers a payment? How will you pay? When will you pay? Say you decide to pay after a salesperson gains two new clients and brings in a revenue of half a million dollars in new sales. Should you pay all the variable part at once, or make monthly payments?

Designing a sales incentives scheme takes time and effort. Trying to skimp on time spent designing it will only cause problems down the road when the scheme doesn't work at its best.

Purpose Of The Incentives Scheme

On the surface, the purpose of the incentives scheme is obvious: To pay sales people for the sales they make. However, there is much more to it than that.

A company that relies on a sales team to convince clients to buy from them, must motivate their sales team to act in ways that are aligned with the company's overall goals.

Every company needs a strategy, and the sales compensation scheme must be aligned with that strategy.

Say for example a company is launching a new product and wants to promote it in a specific region. The sales scheme must encourage sales people to prioritize that goal and work towards it. The company must decide on the exact objectives to be reached. For example, is it more important to land profitable deals, or to land new clients even if the profits are cut a bit? Is it best if sales people are motivated to sell to their target, or to sell above it?

Incentives schemes are not simply paying money for making sales. There are many different aspects of the overall goal that must be taken into account.

In this paper we're going to look at what must be taken into account when deciding upon the scheme, and dive deeper into how companies can make the best decision for their objectives.

There Are Many Types Of Incentives

There are many types of incentives schemes to choose from, including commission bases, bonuses, team bonuses and point systems to name just a few.

The incentives scheme provides a framework for the calculation of payments. Let's look at some examples.

Say a company decides that each sales role should be paid $60,000 a year with a fifty/fifty split between fixed and variable portions. Each sales person then receives $30,000 a year as a basic salary.

Now let's suppose management decides that in order to qualify for the other $30,000, the sales person must bring $400,000 in new revenues. The remaining $30,000 might be delivered as:

- A $30,000 bonus at the end of the year, if the $400,000 target was met.
- A commission of seven percent on each sale, up to $30,000.
- No commission for the first $100,000 of revenue, but a payment for each sale after the first $100,000.

These are just some of the options a business might choose from.

Introducing The Two Most Common Incentives Schemes: Bonuses and Commissions

In my experience, bonuses and commissions are the two most common sales incentives schemes. In a moment, we're going to dig deep into these two incentives schemes, using the six factors outlined above. This will give you a practical look at how different factors affect the incentives design process.

Let's Start With The Basics. What Are Bonuses And What Are Commissions?

A **bonus** is a lump sum awarded at a certain time of year. The bonus amount is based on many factors, both quantitative and qualitative. Sales people know when a bonus will be paid. However, the bonus amount is not written into a specific policy and as such bonuses can vary widely from what was expected. For example, if a sales person brings many new clients, but the company suffers unexpected losses, the bonus will not be as high as the sales person hoped.

A **commission** on the other hand is a more structured system which sets out exactly what a sales person receives in return for selling specific amounts. Commissions can be paid monthly, quarterly or annually. Commissions are not necessarily based on percentages, as many people mistakenly believe, such as eight percent of every sale made. They can also be fixed sum payments such as $1,000 for every contract signed.

The Importance Of Selecting The Right System

At first glance, bonuses and commissions might not seem that different. After all, at the end of the day it's all about offering sales people money to motivate them.

However, the way incentives are paid matters a lot to the company.

For example, if a sales team is told they will get a quarterly bonus if they land a new client, that sets out the expectation that teamwork is more important than individual achievements.

If on the other hand, a sales person is offered specific commissions based on defined targets, they know that the target is the important part.

The money each incentive scheme pays might be the same, but each type of scheme fits a different purpose and encourages sales people in different ways.

For example, if an organisation is selling a low-cost packaged software that takes around three months to sell, a commissions model works well because the sales person can simply keep pursuing more and more targets and earning more commission. A yearly bonus would not provide enough motivation.

On the other hand, if the sale is of a complex IT solution that takes many months to close a deal on and involves a team of sales people, support people, IT specialists etc., working towards a quarterly bonus could be just the right incentive.

How To Design A Sales Incentives Scheme

A sales compensation scheme is not an abstract idea, but rather a complex technical system. By taking all the right factors into account, it becomes easier to design and implement the system.

START WITH THREE KEY TECHNICAL ASPECTS

It's easy to get lost in the technical aspects of building a sales scheme, but essentially, they can be boiled down to three key points. These points are an excellent starting point for anyone looking to design a sales scheme.

- Decide which roles are eligible for sales compensation. As I said above, sometimes it's not just the sales people but also supporting roles.

- Decide on the total compensation per sales role. Note, I didn't say a sales person, but rather a sales role. Each role is linked to a compensation plan and though this might be tweaked to suit individual sales people, the overall compensation per sales role should be consistent throughout the company.

- Decide the right mixture between basic salary and incentives. For example, a straight fifty/fifty split where $50,000 is basic salary, with a further $50,000 tied to meeting targets.

Once these three technical elements have been decided, it becomes easier to design a sales scheme based around them.

FOLLOW FOUR VITAL STEPS

Once the three technical aspects above have been taken care of, it's time to dive a bit deeper into the purpose of the sales scheme, and its technical aspects. Start with these four vital steps.

Step One: Know The Objectives

99

As mentioned above, the incentives scheme must support the company's overall strategy. That's why the first step in designing a scheme is to analyse the current and future objectives of the company. This includes quantitative goals such as bringing a certain amount of profit, but must also include qualitative goals such as increasing market share, penetrating new markets, and landing new customers.

The deeper the understanding of the company's goals, the easier it is to decide which kind of behaviours to motivate in the sales team.

Step Two: Delineate Sales Roles

Sales teams can be complex. There may be multiple sales roles, along with supporting groups. The sales cycle might be light and short or it might be long and complex.

It's vital that every person in the team understands their role and responsibilities. Each role must be clearly delineated so there can be no confusion over what each person should do. Furthermore, managers must decide how much sales credit each person is entitled to for their part in closing a deal. For example, if a consultant or someone involved in presales helps land a deal, managers must decide how much they will be compensated.

Step Three: Decide The Payment Mix

Following on from step two, managers must decide on the exact payment mix by role. The key question is what to pay sales people, but managers must also decide what, if anything, to pay as commission to those with a supporting role.

It is best to decide the payment mix at a company-wide level, to keep the scheme consistent. Of course, there is always scope to treat each sales person differently if need be, but this can lead to confusion. A stable company-wide scheme is by far the best option.

The right decision can vary depending on everything from industry standards to examining the current workings of the company.

Managers must also decide how to split compensation between fixed and variable portions. The fixed part is guaranteed no matter the performance while the variable part is tied to how well the sales person meets their targets.

Step Four: Find The Formula

The fourth step is to find the mathematical formula that takes the objectives of the company and translates them into a workable sales compensation scheme.

There are many ways to form the system, mathematically speaking. For example, it might pay out based on revenues, profit, or number of new clients found. It might pay out at any level, or only after a sales person reaches forty percent of their overall target.

How To Choose Between A Commission Or Bonus System

Although there are many kinds of incentives scheme (and we'll cover some of those shortly), commissions and bonuses are the most commonly used, so an in-depth look at how to choose between them is useful.

TAKE THESE SIX FACTORS INTO ACCOUNT

Six key factors to take into account when making the choice are:

- The type of sales roles in the company
- The sales process
- The organisation's culture, maturity and current market position
- Current market conditions, opportunities and challenges
- Company objectives and goals
- The relationship between sales people and clients

Even schemes that look similar on the outside still have unique mechanics. Some schemes are better suited to a company than others, depending on the factors outlined above.

To give you a better idea of how to choose a scheme, I'm going to analyse commissions versus bonuses, using the six factors outlined above.

1. The Type Of Sales Roles In The Company

It's important to be aware of the type of sales roles in your company. Here are some characteristics of sales roles that push a company towards one system or the other.

A bonus system works if:

- The focus is more on team achievements than on individual achievements.
- There are many people involved in closing the sale, so the sole responsibility doesn't rest with one sales person.
- The skill of the sales people isn't the only deciding factor in whether a sale goes through – there are other elements such as market conditions which influence the decision makers.
- Sales people are working in unequal and dissimilar territories that display different growth. Regions have very different targets and the effort needed to reach targets varies widely.

A commission system works if:

- Sales people have a direct influence on the customer's decision to purchase.
- The sales team are highly independent and work to their own individual objectives.
- Sales roles have clear targets, with success being measured in numbers (such as sales brought) rather than milestones (such as new territories entered).
- Territories are similar, require roughly equal effort to sell to, and afford sales people equal opportunities to earn commissions.

2. The Sales Process

Sales processes vary widely between companies, markets, and even territories. The way the sales process works has a direct effect on which type of incentives scheme works best.

A bonus system works if:

- The sales cycle is long (two or even three years) and involves a lot of effort at every stage of the sales process.

- Success is heavily reliant on teamwork and there is a complex network of people and departments involved in closing the sale. For example, the sales process might start with a marketing team that creates campaigns and sells the idea, followed by direct input from both sales people and stakeholders to further educate clients. Pre-sales teams, consultants, specialists and others are all involved in providing value to the client and steering them towards the sale.

- Territories are sufficiently dissimilar that using a commission system is problematic. Sales people don't have the same opportunity to make commissions even if they have equal skills and are selling the same product. A bonus system can be used to compensate for the problems that come with dissimilar territories.

- Targets and goals are not easy to quantify and there isn't much data available for evaluation. A bonus system makes it easier to evaluate performance based on qualitative factors as well as more concrete ones.

A commission system works if:

- The sales cycle is short (days, weeks, or a couple of months).
- Off-the-shelf products and solutions that don't require customized solutions for each customer, rather than complex bespoke offerings.
- The success or lack thereof in reaching targets is one of the most important aspects of measuring sales success and sales person performance.
- Sales performance is easy to measure.
- Sales people focus most of their efforts on the selling process and don't have to spend a lot of time on non-sales tasks.
- Sales people are not expected to extend their role to include invoicing, implementation, troubleshooting or account management.

- Rewards are tied to the signing of a contract or the purchase of a product.

3. The Organisation's Culture, Maturity And Current Market Position

Every organisation has its own culture, and occupies a unique market position. These factors, along with the maturity of the company and its reputation, can influence which sales scheme is best.

A bonus system works if:

- Each sales person performs a range of roles within the company and has responsibilities that extend beyond selling. Sales people perform tasks such as invoicing and post-sales implementation, but are not paid for those tasks.
- The cost of incentives is hard to forecast because they depend on the performance of sales people in any given period. If sales surpass budgeted targets, then commissions would also surpass expense forecasts, which could lead to the organisation making a greater payout than intended. A bonus, on the other hand, can be capped at a certain amount.

A commission system works if:

- The company relies heavily on sales people rather than alternative channels such as marketing, digitized sales or indirect selling to bring in new sales.
- The company wants to keep sales people motivated to reach and exceed targets. A commission system makes it easier to offer large earning potential without caps on the amount that can be earned.
- The company wants to control how much the compensation scheme costs. A commission-based system is easier to quantify and the company can set payment rules to control the expenses. For example, the system can be designed to pay a certain amount of earnings, so managers know commissions won't rise above a certain amount.

4. Current Market Conditions, Opportunities And Challenges

Every market is different in terms of opportunities, maturity, and unique challenges. An incentives scheme that works for one market won't necessarily work for another.

A bonus system works if:

- The company has expanded into a new region and wants to explore the market and see what kind of market share is a feasible target.
- The market is in crisis and revenues are hard to generate – in such cases the goals may shift from increasing revenues to customer retention, and high commission-based targets become hard to reach.

A commission system works if:

- The company has already tested the waters in a new market and is ready to take a market share in that region.
- The market is stable and well known with clearly defined opportunities.
- The organisation has a mature presence and strong reputation in the market.

5. Company Objectives And Goals

Every company has unique objectives and goals in terms of revenues, growth, and even company culture and the kind of sales team they want to build. Different incentives schemes suit different objectives.

A bonus system works if:

- There is already a commission system in place that rewards sales people for specific tasks, but management wants sales people to perform additional tasks. An extra bonus can be used to extend the commission plan and encourage sales people to take on other tasks. The company gets the sales team working on a range of tasks to meet their objectives, and the sales team knows they will be rewarded for those tasks.

A commission system works if:

- The company is mostly focused on short term objectives.
- Its objectives are directly related to revenue generation rather than strategic objectives such as profitability or relationship building.
- The company's philosophy focuses on "sell as many units as possible."

6. The Relationship Between Sales People And Clients

Every sales team and every individual sales person has a different relationship to their clients. The nature of this relationship affects which kind of incentives scheme is best.

A bonus system works if:

- The product or service generates extra revenues on a regular basis without significant effort from the sales person. For example, if a service is consumption based and the client uses more and buys more, revenue goes up without direct effort from the sales person. The fact that the client is using more and more of the service might be due to the work of other team members such as support or customer service staff.

A commission system works if:

- Success is based on individual success and the main deciding factor on whether a contract gets closed Is the individual sales person's skill in closing the deal.
- The individual relationships between sales people and clients are key to opening the door to new accounts.

When deciding on the best incentives scheme, it's important to take all of these factors into account. No one factor is more important than the others, and it's important not to base the decision on one of the six factors alone.

Even if one factor strongly suggests a specific system is best, the company must still take all factors into account and look at the combined picture.

Weighing The Benefits And Disadvantages

As with any decision, it's important to weigh up the benefits and disadvantages of any incentives scheme before implementing it. This isn't a trivial decision – the choice of scheme has wide ranging implications, as we have seen.

Having worked in a wide variety of sales environments over the years I've noticed some themes when it comes to benefits and disadvantages.

Here are some of the key things I've noticed.

Commissions Give More Control

Companies that have a commission plan find it easier to guide a sales person's activities. After all, a sales person is driven by the chance to earn more money, and the commission system incentivizes sales activities. For example, if the biggest commission opportunities are tied to selling a specific product, the sales person will focus on that.

Bonuses Are Better For Role Expansion

The above is all well and good, but what if the sales company wants its sales force to perform extra activities? Because those activities are not part of the commission plan, sales people are not motivated to do them.

If the company wants to expand sales roles to include non-sales and unpaid activities, a bonus system provides reassurance to sales people that they will be rewarded for all their efforts and not just for direct selling.

Commissions Work Best For Individual Targets

I've noticed that commission-based systems promote a very individualized approach on the part of the sales people. They focus not on their team or company as a whole, but on meeting and exceeding their individual targets.

For companies who want sales people to reach for high targets, or who have clearly defined goals in mind, this is a perfect fit.

Bonuses Work Better For Broader Targets

For some companies, individual sales are not the primary target. A company with a strong growth strategy that includes, for example, customer retention, or providing

107

excellent follow up and support to existing customers, will struggle to implement a commission system. After all, how do you quantify and reward customer care?

In such cases, a bonus plan might work better as it encourages sales people to think about more than hitting targets.

Commissions Work Well When There Is A Direct Relationship Between Effort and Payment

I've found that commissions provide a wonderful motivator in situations where the sales person can see clearly the relationship between their effort and the payment. If it is obvious that their sales strategy leads directly to the sale and thus to the commission, the sales person is motivated to keep hitting and exceeding targets.

Bonuses Work Well When Sales and Payment Are Not Directly Related

There are situations where sales and payment are not so directly related. For example, if many people are involved in closing the sale, or there is a long sales cycle, it's not so easy to see how sales efforts and overall revenue tally up. In such cases it may be better to use a bonus scheme to reward the overall effort of a larger team of people across a range of areas.

The Consequences Of Choosing The Wrong Scheme

Make no mistake; the wrong incentives system can have deep and wide-ranging effects on a company. It's not scaremongering to say that the wrong choice of scheme could cause a company to fail. Let's take a look at some of the most worrisome consequences of choosing the wrong scheme.

Reduced Motivation

The wrong scheme can lead to a demotivated sales force. For example, if a sales person is involved in the overall sales strategy and has many tasks to perform on top of direct selling, a commission scheme could leave them feeling disgruntled. A commission scheme only rewards direct sales, so they might feel their efforts in other areas are for nothing.

Another example might be top earning sales people who love the commissions scheme because it pays handsomely when they meet or exceed their targets. If their company switches to a bonus scheme, they might take a pay cut or even see colleagues putting in less effort, yet getting equally rewarded.

High turnover in the sales force is bad news for a company. As well as the cost of recruiting and training new sales people, there is the fact that until they settle into their role there is likely to be a period of reduced momentum and reduced sales. An incentives scheme that brings down motivation can lead to higher turnover. That is why managers must take the effect of the scheme on the sales people into account when designing it.

Rising Costs

The wrong scheme can cost an organisation a lot of money.

The good news is that cost is not usually a problem with bonus systems because it's easy to set out the budget for the bonus at the beginning and thus limit the amount that will need to be paid. The only question is how to divide the bonus between employees.

Commission systems, on the other hand, can quickly push costs up. If a commission system doesn't have a cap on it, costs can quickly rise.

If there is no provision for exceeding targets, for example, a little over-achievement in the sales force can lead to a big over-payment problem for management. That is why it's important to take extra care when designing commission systems so as not to land the company with unexpectedly high payments.

Poor Sales Results

The wrong incentives scheme has a direct impact on sales results.

Say for example a company motivates its sales people to reach over seventy of their targets because that's the sweet spot where every new sale becomes very profitable. If they want to offer extra incentives to sales staff who bring seventy five percent of their target or more, the wrong incentives scheme makes that very difficult to do.

If the company has a commission system, it's quite easy to adjust it to reward high achievers. However, if the company has a bonus system it's hard to work extra incentives into that. As a result, sales people won't be motivated to reach above their targets, and the company won't get the sales results it needs.

Negative Effects On Company Culture

The wrong incentives scheme can have long term negative effects on the culture of the company, which can jeopardize future profitability, sales and staff morale.

An effective sales scheme needs to do three things:

1. Motivate sales people to act in ways that benefit the company and fit with its objectives.

2. Fit in with both the strategy of the company and the culture it wants to create.

3. To function as a tool managers can use to encourage sales people to perform specific tasks.

The culture of a company covers the principles it operates under and the ethos of the organisation as a whole.

A company that builds a culture of treating sales people as important assets, rewarding them with a better than average salary and great benefits, and showing their appreciation for all they do, is far more likely to succeed.

Sales people who feel valued and rewarded for their efforts are much more likely to stay.

In some cases, a commission system works to build a positive culture, where the focus is on directly rewarding individual sales efforts. For other companies, a bonus system is the better choice as it encourages teamwork and rewards staff for peripheral duties.

Whichever system you use, keep all the potential consequences in mind when choosing.

Operational Factors To Keep In Mind When Choosing An Incentives System

As we've seen, there are many factors to keep in mind when choosing an incentives system. We've outlined the six key considerations above; however, it's also important to keep the following operational factors in mind:

- **Calculation of payments**. Commission systems require more time and effort to calculate, and there is more data to process. This isn't a reason to avoid using them, but companies must make sure they have the resources to handle incentive calculations, and that the team in charge of calculations has access to all the right data.

- **Communication between managers and staff**. Commission systems require a more detailed explanation and training so the staff fully understands how the scheme works, and how they are expected to work within it. Companies must make sure someone is responsible for communication and training, and that it is completed effectively.

- **Territory and quota management**. The balance between the commissions available in each territory, and the quota each sales person must meet, is a delicate one. Managers must be mindful that sales people are equally rewarded for equal effort, even if the territories in question are quite different.

- **Level of staff involvement**. People from various teams will be involved in the incentives scheme. Some will design it, while others manage it, arrange payments, or give exemptions. Companies must think carefully about how the scheme will be administered, who will need to be involved, and what their roles will be.

Alternatives To The Bonus Or Commission Models

I chose to focus on the bonus and commission models because they are by far the most commonly used incentives schemes. However, there are other schemes to choose from. Here is a quick summary of the different schemes a company might explore if it does not feel the bonus or commission model is right for them.

Points Systems

A points system allocates points to sales people based on their performance. The more points a sales person accumulates, the more money they receive. Each achievement is granted a certain number of points according to a pre-defined structure set out by the company.

Managers decide on "point bands" so that points falling within a certain range attract a specific size of payout, points in the next range attract a bigger payout and so on. Points can be allocated for both quantitative and qualitative activities.

Individual Commissions

In some cases, a company might need a modified commissions system. I am often asked how a single commission system can apply to every sales person in the team. The best way to look at it is this: The commission system is linked to a sales role, not to individual people. There could be many people performing the same sales role.

However, there are cases where individual sales people require their own unique commission system. This is usually when their individual territories or responsibilities are so different to other team members that trying to fit them into the standard commission system would lead to them being treated unfairly.

Pool Group Incentives

In pool group systems, all incentives monies (whether bonuses or commissions) are put into one "pot." The pot is then distributed between the members of the sales team.

In such a case, sales people might gain rewards for activities that weren't linked to their efforts to close a deal. This doesn't work for all companies, but there are cases where a concerted team effort is needed to achieve success, and in those cases such a scheme encourages staff to work together.

Hybrid Systems

It's possible to use both bonus and commission systems together. For example, a business might choose to use commissions to motivate the sales team to close deals, but use bonuses for staff whose role, though vital, doesn't directly influence buying decisions.

Another example: A company might choose to use a bonus system up to a certain level of performance, and then commissions above and beyond that. A sales person could receive a bonus up to a hundred percent of their target, but get commissions on anything over a hundred percent of their target, providing an extra motivation to achieve beyond their allocation.

An organisation might also use a bonus system for more qualitative achievements such as customer retention, but choose to run a commission system in parallel for easily quantifiable achievements such as direct sales.

Payment Per Unit

This is a variation on a standard commission system. Usually, a commission system pays out for targets achieved. Targets are usually certain revenue numbers, or profitability-based.

However, sometimes neither revenues nor profitability are the main priority. Perhaps the focus is on bringing in new accounts. In such cases, the company can choose to pay per "units of sale." Sales people get a fixed amount for every client signed to a service or every product sold.

Organisations should be aware that not all sales are profitable sales, and must take this into account when implementing a payment per unit system.

MBO / KSO

MBO / KSO stands for Management By Objectives and Key Sales Objectives.

Simply put, a KSO (key sales objective) is an objective set by management for sales people. A KSO is usually a strategic or qualitative achievement. It is easily measurable and normally paid in units.

For example, a KSO could be to sell a new product in an untouched territory. Such objectives aren't usually stand-alone but are part of a bigger system. Management can take objectives into account when deciding how to pay incentives.

Custom Systems

Organisations also have the scope to improvise and create their own systems. However, I would like to offer a word of caution: Test the new system thoroughly to ensure no mistakes are made. Errors can hit a company hard both in terms of direct cost and in customer turnover, so any custom system must be carefully planned.

Conclusion

Many of my observations are based on my own experience in the technology sector and the sales incentives schemes I've seen in place.

Most companies in my industry favour a commission plan. However, across other industries it's common to see different sales motivation schemes that are more flexible than traditional commission-based systems. Companies also add in elements such as gamification, bonuses and non-monetary rewards such as trips or extra benefits.

One thing is certain: Nearly all companies use their incentives scheme as a tool to manage and guide sales behaviour, and they are right to do so. The incentives scheme is a major factor in relationships between management and employees, from the initial interview and job offering onwards.

As we've seen here, a sales incentives scheme is based on many different factors. The key to implementing a successful scheme is to take all the different factors into account.

Although bonuses and commissions are the most common, there are many different ways to design and use an incentives scheme. An organisation should start by carefully considering their long and short term strategies and the function of each sales role, so they can best choose a scheme that supports their objectives and encourages a healthy, motivated culture and staff.

Performance Measures And Their Weight. Which Are The Main Objective Types To Set To A Sales Role And How To Get The Right Mixture Working For The Team

The Importance Of Your Sales Incentives Plan

Every single company that offers a product or service to the world wants that product to sell. Every financial year-end, companies worldwide look at their figures to see how much they made, and spent, in that year.

There are many factors in a company's success, but there's no doubt that profitability is a huge deciding factor. As a general rule, the more a company sells, the better its chances of being profitable. The more profitable it becomes, the better its chances of future success. And what is the backbone of profitability? Sales.

This is a simplification of course. There are many other factors such as the quality of the product itself, the market, and how well the product is promoted. But even if all of those conditions are ideal, the product itself still needs to actually sell. Customers need to part with their money to buy it.

In order to sell, a company needs a sales plan and channels (such as physical stores or e-commerce), and a sales team. They need their sales people promoting and selling their products to market. The role of sales people cannot be overstated, since their main objective is to sell enough for the company to succeed. For example, if a company decides that in the next year it wants to increase revenues by fifteen, the burden of responsibility falls largely on the sales team.

This is where your sales incentives plan comes in. Psychology and motivation are major factors in your sales team's performance. How can you motivate a sales person to reach their target, and perform beyond it? How can you motivate them to take that sixty percent of their target reached and turn it into a hundred percent?

The answer is your sales incentives plan. The way you design the plan and the technical features you choose can quite literally elevate or jeopardize your company's chances of sales and success.

Performance Measures: A Key Part In The Design Of A Sales Incentives Scheme

There are many moving parts in a sales compensation scheme, including which sales roles are part of the plan, how much cash compensation the scheme pays, and how much of that money is a fixed salary and how much variable.

Another factor that needs serious consideration is the performance measures. These are the key metrics used to set out what the company is asking the sales people to do. Performance measures provide an incentive by helping sales people understand their targets, and how their success will be measured.

Sales managers also need to decide which specific performance measures to use. The alternative is leaving sales people to choose their own performance measures, and that's not effective for the sales team, or for the company.

Most companies would love it if their sales team could magically land new clients, bring new revenues, retain existing clients, cross sell new products to those clients, and promote new products, all at once. But realistically, no sales team can focus on so many different things at one time. It would be impossible to prioritize properly.

Choosing specific performance measures helps a sales team prioritize and put their energy on the tasks that matter most to the company.

There are many different measures to choose from, and selecting the right ones can be tricky. Let's take a closer look at how performance measures work within a sales scheme, and then talk about why choosing the right ones is so important, and how to do that.

When To Choose Your Performance Measures

It's important to remember that deciding on your performance measures isn't the first step to take when designing a sales scheme. Rather, it's better to start by deciding which sales roles are included in the scheme, and how much you'll pay for both the fixed and variable part of the fee.

Once you know who will be paid, how much, and what percentage of the budget goes to the variable component of the sales scheme, it's time to decide on which performance measures to use.

Choosing Performance Measures In A Sales Incentives Scheme

A friend of mine who's a sales manager called me for assistance designing his sales scheme. He told me:

"I started thinking how much to pay my sales people, but then dozens more questions came to mind. Who should get paid? How much should they get paid? Should I pay a variable that's equal to the fixed salary? Do I pay a bonus or commission? At what performance level do I start paying more? And how do I measure their performance to know when to start paying them the variable? I know I want them to focus on selling our newly launched product, but we've also struggled to retain revenues from our existing clients. I don't know where to start!"

I told him that actually, he'd just answered his own question. The best performance measures are the ones that are completely aligned with company strategy. For example, if he wanted to give his sales team an incentive to get existing accounts renewed, he could build that right into his incentives scheme.

For example, he might:

- Allocate existing accounts to members of his sales team.

- Measure the yearly revenues coming in from those accounts.

- Either arrange an incentive payment for sales people who retain a certain percentage of the portfolio (for example, a certain dollar amount for those retaining eighty percent of the portfolio or more), or pay a percentage on each contract they get renewed.

Performance measures are a key part of sales scheme design, because they drive sales team behaviour. A sales incentives plan is a sales management tool that helps managers motivate their team, and reach their objectives. Another example of how to include performance measures in the plan might look like this:

Each sales person should aim to bring in ten new clients this year, create $200,000 in new revenue, and retain $1 million worth of existing business.

In this example, the incentives scheme is built around three specific measures:

1. Landing new clients

2. Bringing in new revenues

3. Retaining existing business

The Importance Of Selecting The Right Performance Measures

The sales incentive scheme drives sales behaviour. Sales people naturally go where the money and extra payments are – that's the whole point of a sales scheme! That's also why you need to make sure you choose the right performance measures. If your performance measures aren't in line with company objectives, sales people won't do the things the company most needs them to do.

Of course, the incentives scheme isn't the only thing that determines sales results. The quality of the product, the fit of product to market, how competitive the market is, how easy a product is to sell, and many other factors, help determine sales.

But the incentives scheme is certainly one important factor, and **choosing the wrong performance measure can lead to problems** such as:

- Misalignment of sales behaviour with the company's objectives

- Results skewed towards the wrong objectives

- Sales people focus on the wrong tasks

- Frustration and lack of motivation in the sales team

Four Rules To Help You Choose The Right Performance Measures

We'll look more closely at different measures in a moment, but let's start with four basic rules that I use to help my team and others choose which performance measures to use:

- Choose measures that are aligned with management objectives (so if management want to increase existing client retention, make percentage of existing clients retained one of your performance measures.)

- Tie measures to anticipated results. For example, if a company promised their shareholders profits and revenues, use profitability and revenue as two main performance measures.
- Make sure territories are fairly and reasonably distributed between sales measures, to make it easier to set performance measures.
- Management must assign targets that are specific to the chosen measures.

Types Of Measures

There are a wide variety of performance measures you can use, and they fall into three main categories:

Quantitative Measures

These can be measured in currency, numbers, amounts or items. Examples include the acquisition of new customers, profit, gross revenues, number of units sold, and so on.

Qualitative Measures

These cannot be counted in the same concrete way as quantitative measures. They include, for example, increasing relationships with new clients, up selling and cross selling, customer retention, customer satisfaction, market share, and so on. These are harder to measure, and thus harder to incentivize.

Qualitative measures fall into three main categories.

Customer related:

- Win back customers
- Improve client satisfaction
- Cross and up sell products
- Replace certain competitors

- Increase market share
- Reach specific milestones with clients

Industry related:

- Penetrate a new industry
- Win new strategic accounts
- Improve awareness in the market
- Bring new products to the market

Territory related:

- Partnership with a certain partner
- Win strategic accounts in a territory
- Increase footprint in territory
- Improve market awareness in a territory

Management Business Objectives (MBOs)

These are milestones for the company, such as winning the first numbers in a new industry (which in this case might be a more significant achievement compared to the actual revenues brought in by doing so.)

A Deeper Look At Qualitative Measures

The use of qualitative measures isn't straightforward. However, I firmly believe that when used thoughtfully and with purpose, they are very effective.

Qualitative measures aren't popular, because they're not easy to quantify and they can be confusing for sales people, both of which are valid concerns. However, in my experience, companies that use them in a carefully planned and designed manner see improvements in their results of more than seventeen percent.

Qualitative measures can support very individual and specific goals, and help sales teams go for those goals. Because they can be very specific, they serve those individual goals in a way that makes a big difference to the company. Using personalized objectives in this way has a big impact. And quite frankly, qualitative measures are interesting to apply and require strategic thinking, which encourages everyone involved to plan and focus more effectively.

Setting qualitative measures is challenging. How can you put a specific target on "improving brand awareness in this specific territory?" There aren't any simple numbers you can allocate. That's why I recommend companies follow these three tips when using qualitative measures:

- Don't use qualitative measures as your core measure. For example, you might measure gains in a new market, but keep your primary measure as a specific revenue dollar amount.
- Don't use more than two qualitative measures at once.
- If you are using two measures, make sure they complement each other and work well together.

A special note for startups: If you're a startup and you're still in that unstable beginning phase, only set one qualitative measure, and for a shorter period of time such as a year or less.

How To Weight Performance Measures

Once you've decided on which performance measures to use, the next step is deciding how much weight each of them has within the incentives scheme. Their weight, or importance, tells you how much money to allocate to them and how much to pay sales people when they reach those targets.

Let's say a company decides to measure performance using new revenues, cross-selling new products, and existing customer retention. They weight it thus:

- New revenues fifty percent
- Cross selling new products twenty five percent
- Existing customer retention twenty five percent

Now they decide that for a hundred percent realization of targets, each sales person on this scheme will get $50,000 annually. The company can now allocate a specific dollar amount to each target:

- $25,000 for new revenues

- $12,500 for cross selling new products

- $12,500 for retaining existing customers

Now the company knows exactly what to pay each sales person per goal achievement, and the sales team knows what their potential earnings are, and what they must do to make that money.

The company can break this down even further. For example, if the yearly goal is to bring five new clients, then the payment for each new client is $2,500. Or, they might choose a system where the first three clients attract a slightly smaller payment, and the final two attract a larger payment, with a combined total of $12,500. The latter strategy shows sales people that the more they achieve, the bigger the payment they get.

Weighting shows sales people how they can make money, which drives their behaviour and determines where they put most of their effort. Carefully considered weighting is a useful tool for getting the company where managers want it to go.

6 Rules For Effective Performance Measure Weighting

As you can see, choosing how to weight performance measures is key to success with performance weighting. Here are six rules that I use with my own clients to make the decision process easier and more effective:

- Use no more than three to five performance measures, so the minimum weight for each measure is not too low. This also stops sales people scattering their attention between too many different things.

- Don't allocate less than ten percent to any measure. Below ten percent simply isn't enough to keep sales people interested in reaching the target.

- Make one or two of your measures the core measures, with at least thirty percent weight each. This tells sales people where to put most of their effort.

- Give the most weight to the measures that will make the biggest impact on an organisation and which are easiest to follow. This makes it easy for sales people to stay focused on important tasks.

- Only give weight to things that can be measured one way or another, whether that's quantitative or qualitative.

- Put most of your weight on revenue and profit generating measures.

It's also a good idea to run hypothetical exercises to see how much the system would pay on each measure and goal in different scenarios, and how often the measures will be achieved. Do this before rolling it out to your sales team so you have a good idea of what the performance measures will look like in practice.

The right sales incentives plan is vital to the success of any business that relies on a sales team. Choosing the right performance measures is a key part of that plan. Always think carefully about the main objectives you need your sales team to focus on, and choose performance measures that directly support those objectives. That way, your sales team will be encouraged to focus on the most useful tasks, and be motivated to meet the goals that best serve your company.

Incentives Mechanics; Caps, Entry Thresholds, Multipliers Are Some Of The Technical Terms One Can Use In An Incentives Scheme. Each One Has Its Unique Purpose

I recently met with the head of sales at a technology company. He managed a team of twenty-five people, and he needed my help because the cost of incentives had risen in the last two years, and was eating most of their profit margins.

He was by no means alone. I meet with many stakeholders who complain their sales incentives scheme is too costly compared to the benefits it gives. On the other hand, some of them insist that the problem must be something other than the scheme, because the scheme couldn't possibly be the problem!

So, where does the truth lie?

Before we look more closely at sales incentives schemes, let's see the problems that arise from an inefficient sales compensation program. Some of the issues my clients raise with me include:

- High sales turnover
- Sales people not meeting targets
- Poor or inconsistent sales results
- Sales people feeling they're not being treated equally
- Low customer retention
- Losing key accounts
- Decreasing market share
- A sense of dissatisfaction among the sales team

All of these can certainly be caused by wrong sales scheme design. I do want to caution against blaming the incentives scheme for everything – don't make it a scapegoat! Not every problem in an organisation is to do with the sales team. It's all too easy to assume the answer to any problem is to give more incentives (which of course then increases overall costs associated with the scheme), or otherwise tinker with the program.

However, if like my client, your sales scheme is increasing in cost and yet not motivating sales people to reach and over-perform their targets, it's always worth sitting down and having a closer look at the design.

It Takes More Than Thirty Minutes To Design An Incentives Program

When I asked my client how the company designed their sales scheme, he asked me what I meant. He told me they'd simply decided that they needed a commission plan, and that commission plan would be a certain payout for up to a hundred percent of target realization, and then a higher payout for people who reached more than a hundred percent of their target.

The team had designed the scheme in less than thirty minutes, put it into practice, and hoped for the best. When I asked if they'd done commission forecasts and made plans for how to allocate the budget if the results differed from the forecast, he couldn't answer.

The design of a sales incentives scheme is vital to the success of any company that relies on sales. When my company surveyed sales people, we discovered that a poor incentives scheme is one of the major reasons sales people leave a company.

A good scheme helps with staff retention, increases the chance of an organisation reaching its targets, and boosts profit margins. To design a scheme that does these things effectively you need a dedicated team, the cooperation of the stakeholders, technical skills, planning, and definitely thirty minutes.

Whether you are designing a sales scheme from scratch, or need to re-design your existing one, this article will walk you through the mechanics involved in designing a sales scheme.

Where To Start

The design of a sales scheme starts with assessing the current situation in the company, and the current system. You need to know what you're working with, so you know where to go next.

It's also vital that you consider the long and short term corporate objectives. This goes beyond sales – wanting sales is obvious – and asks the big questions of where does the company want to be in five years' time? How do they want to be perceived by their clients? What kind of market share do they want to have?

Once you have your objectives set, consider the role that sales people will play in reaching those objectives. What precisely do management want their sales people to do? Is it their main aim to create new markets? Build new long-lasting relations with clients? Retain existing clients?

It starts by assessing the current situation in the company and the current system in place. It is critical that one also considers carefully the corporate objectives in the short and the long term. What does the company try to achieve; not just selling its product to the market and win some business obviously. What is the dream? How do they want their clients to perceive the company in five years' time?

The next step is deciding how much cash compensation the company wants to pay. This needs to be split between the fixed part of the scheme, and the variable part.

Once the aims, sales team goals, and compensation figures are decided upon, it's time to get into the nitty gritty of designing the sales scheme mechanics.

Four Rules To Apply When Considering Mechanics

Designing a sales scheme can quickly get complicated. If you keep these four main rules in mind throughout the process, things will go a lot more smoothly:

- Don't over complicate things. If the sales scheme is too confusing, your sales team will find it confusing to use. The more difficult it is to understand, the less effective it will be.

- Always keep the sales person's point of view in mind when designing the scheme. Ask how the scheme will be perceived and if it's easy to use. Make sure the scheme fits with the company culture.

- Make sure the sales compensation mechanics work well together and don't contradict each other.

- Make sure you don't accidentally use too many different mechanics in order to bring the same results, as this can get needlessly complicated. Use only as many mechanics as you need.

Mechanics To Use In An Incentives Program

Below you'll find a comprehensive list of mechanics you can use in your incentives plan. **The key here is not to try and use them all at once!** Too many different mechanics leads to over complication. You might also find that the reasons for using a specific mechanic aren't always obvious.

For example, the first mechanic on the list below is the cap. That means the maximum payment any sales person can reach, no matter how highly they perform. Some people mistakenly think that means a cap can be used to control the pay of one particular sales person who is in danger of over performing. However, that's an unfair way of using it, and likely to lead to resentment. It makes more sense to use the same cap across the sales force, to prevent unexpected mega orders, which if not capped could lead to higher payouts than the company can support.

Let's take a closer look at the different mechanics of a sales scheme:

Caps

The cap sets a maximum payout for sales staff no matter how much they exceed their targets.

Some companies use a hard cap, which means there are no exceptions. However, some prefer a soft cap, which leaves management free to pay a bonus above the cap level at their own discretion.

The benefit of using a cap is that the company knows in advance what its maximum payout will be. A cap also limits the potential earning gap between team members. It also means that mega orders or unexpected orders can't cause a financial disaster.

There are some bad sides too, however. Sales people don't respond well to caps as they want to feel the sky is the limit. Because of this, a cap must be used very carefully.

If at all possible, I suggest using one of these alternatives to a cap:

Setting up quotas to minimize the chances of over-performance and therefore over-payment.

Introduce a policy that payments above a certain amount are at the discretion of a specific committee, so sales people know that certain high earnings will need to be assessed and a decision made.

Use an alternative incentives payout for realization above the hundred percent of targets. For example, paying commissions as usual up to a hundred percent but then switching to a bonus system that gives extra payments without the same risk of unusually high payouts.

Use regressive ramped commissions that mean the higher a sales person goes above their target, the lower the commission rates.

Write a specific policy to handle mega orders that sets out how extra large orders are to be handled, outside of the core incentives system. That way sales people know their normal earnings won't be capped, and are more likely to be understanding of the fact that mega orders are assessed using different rules.

The best time to use a cap: When you have many unexpected big deals that are happening in a year.

Linkage Of Measures

Most sales incentives plans have more than one performance measure. For example, a sales person might have a target to bring a certain amount of revenue for product X, and then a different amount of revenues for product Y.

Linkage of measures means that one measure effects the other. For example, the payment for meeting the product X target will only happen after the performance target for product Y is also achieved.

Using a linkage is a good way to give sales people a strong message about the main priority of the business. Too many linkages can get confusing for sales people. In our example here, even if they excel as selling product X, they'll understand that they need to bring their A game to their product Y sales too now, because both payments are linked.

There are two main ways to use linkage: Hurdle or multiplier. Let's take a closer look at each.

A hurdle is like our example above. Payment is released only if both performance targets are met. Hurdles are not well liked by sales people, and with good reason. It leaves them feeling that even if their performance in one area is outstanding, they'll still be penalized if they don't reach targets in the other area. A hurdle is good for helping sales people set their priorities and shows which is their main target. However, the negative aspects must also be taken under consideration.

A multiplier is a different type of linkage that doesn't penalize sales people in the way hurdles do. Instead, the incentives value of one measure (let's call it target A) increases or decreases in relation to another measure (let's call it target B). So, if a sales person succeeds in target A they'll be rewarded, but if they succeed in target B too, they'll be rewarded even more handsomely. The main challenge when adding a multiplier linkage to a sales scheme is budgeting for the cost of the linked incentives. One way to avoid the risk of overpaying is to offer half the full commission rate for a target, and then use a multiplier to take it up to the full budgeted amount if targets are met.

When to use linkage of measures: When you want to make sure a specific measure gets prioritized. Using linkage makes sure sales people must prioritize the right measures.

Matrices And Grids

Matrices and grids are used to combine two sales measures and allocate different percentages to them, depending on the common achievement of different levels in two measures.

Say for an example, a grid is used to determine how the combined effort across two different sales performance measures will work. Management might decide that if a sales person achieves fifty percent in both revenue target performance AND profit margin, then the sales person will receive a commission rate of seven percent. However, if they achieve ninety percent profit margin performance, the commission is fourteen percent.

Matrices can be confusing and sales people might find it difficult to absorb exactly how they work. However, they are an efficient way to combine two performance measures and incentivize the common achievement of both while penalizing low combinations.

Grids and matrices aren't that common but can be very effective. The key to making them work is to make sure that both the measures are important to the company, and that the sales person has the capacity to affect both measures.

When to use grids and matrices: When you need to be sure your sales force succeeds in more than one measure at the same time.

Entry Threshold

Entry threshold is the mechanic which is used to indicate the lowest performance level at which a sales person can receive a payment. For example, management might decide that commissions will only be paid once a sales person reaches thirty percent of their target.

Entry thresholds can be used on any number of measures within a system. They're normally used for roles that have a fixed salary. The thinking behind mechanics is that the salary for a sales role brings with it the expectation of a certain minimum performance level. An entry threshold means sales people need to meet this minimum performance level if they want to get paid.

When setting an entry threshold, it's important to choose the right level. If the threshold is too high, sales people could become de-motivated and feel like even if they work hard, they won't get paid.

A threshold of more than thirty or forty percent is too high for most companies. In addition, it can sometimes be helpful to have a discretionary policy whereby sales people who are just a couple of percent off their target will still get paid if management agrees to it.

When to use entry thresholds: When you know that some results will come independent of the sales person's work and skills. You can also use them when you expect that for the salary you give you will get a certain amount of results.

Pay Based On Weighted Performance In All Measures

When a company has more than one key objective, it can be hard to figure out how to ensure the sales force works on all of those objectives. In order to avoid confusions among the team, try to cap different objectives at three to five per sales person.

Once you have your objectives set, however, how do you make sure your sales people meet all of them, instead of just sticking with the one or two they feel most comfortable with?

One way to do this is to use a weighted performance of all measures, and then pay according to the percentage of the weighted average. This is an elegant alternative to the other mechanics listed above, which allows management to assign weight to different measures at different times, according to company priorities. To achieve a high weighted average, a sales person must work to achieve their goals across all measures and objectives.

One downside to this mechanic is that it can be confusing for sales people. It can also negatively affect motivation for sales people who are stronger in some areas than others, because they feel like they're being penalized for failures instead of recognised for successes.

When to use pay based on weighted performance in all measures: Use this when it's important that the sales force works on multiple measures or objectives at the same time.

Differentiators

Differentiators mean that the payout received by a sales person varies depending on how the objective is met.

For example, I worked with a company whose sales people were selling new products to their existing clients, and the full range of products to new clients. The company was suffering from a lack of new clients in the last few years. The reason was that sales people had no incentive to sell to new clients. New clients needed more stamina and a different strategy. It was more effort, for the same payout as they'd get selling to existing clients, which was easier. We decided that what the company needed was a differentiator – a little something extra for sales people who sold to new clients. Now their team had a reason to make the extra effort to sell to new clients.

Here are some other examples of ways to apply differentiators:

- Paying differently if a client is a strategic client, a particularly desirable account, or belongs to a group that the company wants to prioritize selling to.

- Paying more to sales people who negotiate a higher sale price on a product and therefore make a bigger profit on the deal.

132

- Paying more if a sales person sells to certain industries, to a certain size of clients if selling to companies rather than individuals, in a specific geographic area, or any other factor that it makes sense to reward.

- Paying more if the sale is to a lost customer, thus winning them back.

- When to use differentiators: When you want to guide people in a specific direction and show them that getting results in specific areas matters more than simply getting results in any area.

Common Problems That Arise When Applying Mechanics

There are some common problems that come up again and again when a company decides and applies its mechanics. Being aware of these will help you avoid them. The examples below are all from clients who requested our help because their sales scheme simply wasn't working.

Misuse of caps: One company we worked with tried to control the cost of incentives by using a cap. The cap was set at just 130 percent and it riled up the sales force. They felt it was unfair, because the targets were not easy to reach, and yet if they put in enough effort to not only reach but to exceed them, they were being penalized rather than rewarded for it. Their best performers were reaching more than 200 percent of some difficult targets, and not being paid for their achievements. In a two-year period, some of the top sales people were leaving the company.

Making weighted measures too hard to achieve: One client was using a weighted measures scheme, and had set the entry threshold at sixty percent across four different measures. That means a sales person had to perform at least sixty percent in weighted performance of four objectives before they had any chance of seeing an incentive payment! Most people were doing well in the majority of the measures but just failing in one, and yet being penalized for it. The system was too hard and as a result the sales staff stopped trying.

Making the linkage system too complicated: One client had three main product lines, each with an individual target. Instead of choosing a primary objective and linking the other two to it, the company had linked all three together. The system was so complicated that most sales people gave up the effort of reaching their targets, because they were spending most of their time trying to decode the system.

Setting targets too low when using multipliers: We've talked about setting targets and thresholds too high, but sometimes setting them too low can be a problem too. One client we worked with had applied a multiplier to all other objectives provided the core objective was met. Unfortunately, so many sales people met their targets that their incentives costs skyrocketed! After some analysis we were able to show them that the core targets were set too low, and needed to be raised.

The mechanics of a sales scheme are the ideal way to give the sales team direction and show them what is expected of them. The right mechanics also reward good performance.

However, as you can see, companies don't always fully assess the consequences a mechanic might have. That's why we recommend taking time to assess how different mechanics might play out in the real world. It's also important to keep in mind that using sales scheme mechanics isn't obligatory. Use only the ones that make sense for your objectives, and that motivate rather than confusing or frustrating your sales people.

How To Deal With Specific Areas Of The Incentives Program – Situations Like Big Tickets, Strategic Account Sales, Renewals, etc. And How To Compensate Sales People For Them

One thing that I will say over and over again because people in this field need to hear it is that an incentives program is not something you can design and administer in a couple of hours. It takes time to design a sales program. At the very least you need to consider not only the plan and incentives themselves, but also:

- The administration of the plan
- Committees involved in running it
- Calculating incentives
- Analysing results
- Communication with sales people and others

There are many different steps and technical aspects to consider.

I often talk about the main things to consider: The sales roles and responsibilities, the target cash compensation, the balance between fixed and variable, and the commission system. However, even after you straighten out all the technical details, there are other things to consider.

These are smaller items that design teams sometimes overlook, because they're not part of the core program. These are the specific items of a plan – all the little additional things that the team needs to have a policy for.

You can't predict every single angle of the system and any problems that might arise within it. However, if you consider each of the specific item, you'll have a smoother system with less risk of glitches.

Indirect Sales Channels

Sometimes a company sells through indirect channels rather than through a sales force. For example, if a company sells direct to supermarkets who then sell on to end customers, then they're using an indirect channel.

The question then is how does one motivate the person who's responsible for selling to an indirect channel? What exactly should their managers motivate them for? How can the company assess that person's performance to decide how to compensate them for selling to an indirect channel?

Sometimes an indirect channel is the first choice for a sale. Sometimes it's not the first choice, but pioneering sales people might expand into indirect selling anyway, by reaching out to retailers, associations, consultants and others.

How To Compensate Sales To Third Party Channels

The challenge here is that managers can't use sales figures as part of the motivation scheme, as they don't have access to data from the third party. Business don't share this information with their suppliers.

In some cases, a company might be able to reach an arrangement with the third party so they can get some sales data from them. Even if this can't be done, companies can still measure how many sales are made to a third-party supplier and how much profit those sales bring.

Using this data to assess third party sales and reward sales people for them keeps them motivated to keep making those sales.

Renewals

Not all sales is to new clients. Some sales people focus on existing clients, while others work with both new and existing clients. For example, a key account manager might deal with both renewing existing contracts and making new sales.

Every company should think about how to motivate their sales team to renew existing contracts.

A couple of years ago I met with the head of sales of a technology company. She believed that sales people responsible for signing new contracts should be paid four times as much as the account managers, who dealt only with renewing contracts. As a result of this policy, renewal rates were falling. Account managers weren't motivated to work hard to get contracts renewed, because they weren't being well compensated compared to people who landed new contracts.

No company can afford to lose business. Renewals means loyal clients, and that's good for profits and reputation both. That's why every company must decide how to compensate sales staff who land contract renewals.

Things To Consider When Designing The Renewals Incentives

Here are some things to consider when deciding what and how to pay for renewals:

Whether a contract is automatically renewed, and how it renews. Automatically renewing contracts take less effort on the part of the sales person and so might be paid less.

How the company realises profits. According to the accounting standards it complies with, how much revenue does this renewal bring?

What type of service or system is being sold, as this can make a difference as to how the system is treated in terms of profits and revenue booking. For example, are we talking about:

- BPaaS
- Recurring revenues from a SaaS service
- A license that doesn't renew automatically
- A multi-year contract
- A rental of service
- A hosting solution
- A managed service
- A consultancy contract

All of these bring different revenues and take a different amount of effort on the part of the sales person to renew.

Renewal tenor. If a sales person manages to renew a contract for more than the standard (for example if the standard is one year but he gets a client to renew for three years at one time), then he needs to get paid more for this.

Analysis of the product at hand. How much revenue is it bringing? And how is that revenue paid? Is it upfront, license, or something else?

Account management role. Is there a special group of account managers dedicated to manage existing relationships and contracts? If this is a strategic initiative from the company then one would need to consider an appropriate level of incentives.

How much the company relies on existing contracts. Is the company operating and selling to an industry where new sales are scarce? Do they rely on existing clients? If this is the case then renewals are a must and this must be recognised.

Effort in account management. How much effort does a sales person make to get a renewal? Does it take a lot of effort to build credibility and trust with the client to get that renewal? If it takes considerable time then it is fair to consider higher renewal payment.

When To Pay Or Not Pay Renewals

Here are some example cases where it might be appropriate to pay, or not pay, for renewals. However, each company is different so please take your own unique situation under consideration.

- If your company recognises revenues year on year because of renewal? Pay for them.
- If there is a high turnover of customers and this is normal for your industry, not a problem to be fixed? Pay a smaller amount for renewals but don't over emphasize them.
- If you don't rely on renewals for profits? Don't incentivize them.
- If there is a specific sales team that deals with account management and renewals? Compensate them for landing those renewals.
- If the core strategy of the company is to sell to existing customers? Pay for renewals.

Big Ticket Sales

Sometimes an unexpected opportunity comes along to make an exceptionally big sale. An unexpected big ticket sale can be costly to the company, so it's a good idea to have a policy in place for those.

Make no mistake – if a big ticket sale is paid according to the usual incentives plan, there's a risk of it running to a six or seven digit commission. That's why companies need to be prepared for how to handle such sales.

Factors To Consider Regarding Big Ticket Sales

There are several things to consider when planning for big ticket sales:

Is there an incentives cap? An incentives cap can prevent big ticket sales, but still allows room for an extraordinary payment at the company's discretion.

How frequent are big ticket sales? It's helpful to know how many big ticket sales come up in an average year, and whether they're random or if there's a bigger pattern, such as bigger tickets in a certain region.

What do the big tickets have in common? As well as region, look at whether certain people are frequently bringing big ticket sales, or if certain products tend to attract them?

How do clients pay for big ticket sales? Do they pay upfront, or are they mostly via licenses, or ongoing professional services? When is the revenue booked from an accounting point of view?

Are big ticket sales desirable? Is the company actively looking for them, or would they rather discourage them? Do they prefer a higher amount of smaller ticket sales, for example?

How does the company want to treat big ticket sales? There's more than one way to handle big ticket sales. A company might choose to:

- Treat them as being outside the main sales scheme.
- Treat them as falling within the system, but have a cap on how much it will pay for them.

- Put a cap on the sales scheme as a whole and include big tickets within that cap.
- Use a cap, but also add a bonus for big ticket items.

The key is to define what exactly counts as a big ticket, and have a consistent policy for how to treat them.

Global/Key/Strategic Accounts

Some bigger organisations categorize their clients into different segments. This is particularly helpful for more mature organisations with lots of clients who need to manage those clients differently.

One common segment is key accounts. These are sometimes called strategic or global accounts.

Key accounts usually have an appointed account manager and are treated differently than other accounts, due to their importance. Every company that has key accounts should decide how to credit incentives for those accounts.

The Complication Of Crediting Key Accounts

Crediting key accounts can be complicated. In many cases there is more than one person involved with these accounts.

For example, there might be one sales person attached to a key account, but another sales person who covers the vertical industry in a specific region. So, who does what, and who gets credit for sales to that account?

The best way to handle this is to have a set policy that outlines how to credit key accounts.

The first step is to define in detail the sales roles and responsibilities for key accounts. Set out clearly who covers these accounts, and their objectives and goals.

Companies need to get very clear on who does what within such an opportunity, and especially who influences the stakeholders and who advances the opportunity towards the sale.

Sales Crediting For Key Accounts

When a key account involves more than one sales person, there are various ways to give sales credit:

- Full payment to one person;
- Full payment to more than one person;
- Partial payment to all sales people involved adding up to a hundred percent of the total; or
- Partial payment to all sales people involved, but not adding up to a hundred percent of the total.

Let's look at an example. Say a strategic account manager normally looks after one or two accounts and their target is to retain those accounts, promote organic growth, and upsell to existing accounts. However, they work alongside product sales managers or country sales managers to build a global relationship.

In this case, management should consider:

- Whether the key account manager has the same targets as other sales people or not.
- How much they rely on internal relationships and other people to get the sale.
- How instrumental they are in driving the client relationship.
- Whether they are generating opportunities.
- Whether they are driving client decisions.

In addition, there is extra complication if any of the following are true:

- They're a global firm that installs services locally but signs centrally in HQ.
- They're a global firm that installs and signs locally without HQ involvement.

- They're a global firm that sells a global solution that will be installed in different locations.

It's better to know in advance how to treat key accounts. I suggest the following three steps to make it simpler:

First, define what is a key / strategic / global account, and which sales people are responsible for them.

Second, draw up a table that outlines the sales team and how they work together on key opportunities.

Third, draw up a table that shows alternatives to sales credit and when it is appropriate to choose each option.

Payment Periods

Every commission needs to include payment periods. Some sales are paid monthly, while others are paid yearly.

In many cases revenue doesn't come straight through to the profit and loss of the company, but rather is accounted for in a later accounting period. This may contradict with how commissions are paid, as commissions are often taken as a straightforward expense in the current period.

For example, let's think about a company that sells a software license. This license includes maintenance and professional services. The client signs a contract that shows they pay their license fee upfront and then pay their annual maintenance fee in three instalments.

However, the incentives for the sales people selling those licenses might be on a different cycle of payment. For example, they might get their full commission as soon as the contract is signed.

It's clear that deciding how to pay incentives when they don't match up with the client payment cycle is complex. One key thing to consider is whether to use a discreet or cumulative system. Let's take a closer look.

Discreet vs Cumulative Systems: How To Choose

A discreet system is one where the system resets for every period. For example, it might have monthly targets and every month starts a new period. A cumulative system is one where incentives can be paid based on a cumulative YTD performance calculation. That performance is measured on a year to date YTD basis.

Managers need to examine how often the system pays and whether to make upfront payments. This means looking at how and when products bring revenues and how that lines up with the incentives program. Part of this is deciding whether to use a discreet or cumulative system.

I recommend using discreet payments when:

- Each period is important.

- There's a short sales cycle.

- Your company sells transactional products rather than complex solutions.

I recommend using cumulative payments when:

- YTD performance is important.

- You want to incentivize yearly performance.

- You want to give sales people the benefit of cumulative achievements.

Additional Factors To Consider When Deciding Payment Periods

Here are some additional factors to keep in mind when deciding which payment period to use.

Products sold. Are they complex with a long sales cycle? Or are they sold relatively quickly and easily?

When revenues are recognised. At what point in the accounting cycle is each revenue recognised?

The types of revenues that are involved. One company might recognise several types of revenue including recurring revenues (with or without automatic renewal), installed software, licenses and one of contracts.

The time needed to compute incentives. If the system is a complex one and needs a lot of data to compute incentives, or if there are dozens of sales people involved, monthly incentives might be hard to manage.

The size of the average sales ticket. If the sales are fast moving and not especially complex, a more frequent payment period can work.

Sales person performance. The number of deals on average a sales person can expect to bring influences the payment period – sales people who go too long without seeing payment will not stay motivated.

Payment timing. Do you want to pay when the contract is signed, or when the client pays the invoice? And does the client pay in arrears or up front?

Current average yearly commissions. Is the company happy with the current commissions paid through the existing system or does something need to change?

In general, a monthly payment works when the sales cycle is long and complex. However, you can always use a bonus system to move the payment into a yearly cycle.

Alternate Sales Credit Points

It's worth looking more closely at the sales credit point. In most cases sales are credited when the client signs a contract. However, there are other options:

- Express of interest from the client – this is a good option in startup environments to encourage sales people to bring leads and opportunities.

- Signature of agreement – this is the standard sales credit point for most companies.

- Invoice sent – this encourages sales people to reach the point of invoicing the client with their efforts.

- Invoice paid – this is helpful when it's especially important to make sure all money is collected from clients.

- End of installation – this can be used to encourage sales people to be involved with the installation process and customer support (but see below for a cautionary tale on how this can backfire.)
- Positive feedback from client – it's rare to wait and pay the full incentive at this point, but paying a partial incentive here can be useful in niche industries and transactional products.

I recently consulted with a company that was paying on installation of the system. However, it was clear from talking to the sales team that they weren't happy with that. They weren't in charge of installation and implementation, yet they had to wait for those to be completed before they were paid.

The company had implemented the system that way to encourage sales people to be more hands on after selling the system, but in reality, the installation team and sales team were heavily fragmented, and the result was the opposite of what was intended.

I suggested the same thing to them that I'm suggesting to you now: Think carefully about how you want to motivate your sales people, and the points at which you want them to make an extra effort. A sales crediting cycle that leaves your sales force disgruntled is a fast track to losing good sales people.

Splitting The Sales Credit

Another option for some companies is to split the sales credit between different points of interest. For example, you might pay fifty percent when the agreement is signed and fifty percent at the end of installation.

However, in this case the sales person needs to have some responsibility for the installation and delivery. As we just saw, making sales people wait for something over which they have no control is not a good motivator.

Another option is to pay part of the commission when the contract is signed and the other part once the client pays. This encourages sales people to follow through on payment – but do be mindful that this can also put sales people into a money collector role, which isn't ideal.

To make your sales crediting decision, I recommend drawing up a simple questionnaire that covers:

- Targets frequency (monthly, quarterly, annually)
- How often to pay (monthly, per deal, annually)
- At which point of interest to pay (signature, payment)
- How to split the payment (e.g. fifty percent signature and fifty percent in payment)

Armed with this, you and your team can put together a sales crediting cycle that makes sense for your company and products, and keeps your sales team motivated.

Draws

Another specific item that needs consideration is the use of draws (upfront payment in advance of performance). Companies are understandably wary about using draws, but there are some circumstances in which they're a viable option.

- When there's a long sales cycle.
- When the financial climate is unstable and sales people need to know they'll get paid even if the current times are uncertain.
- When there's a high pay at risk in the variable part of the compensation scheme, and a degree of uncertainty surrounding it.
- To motivate newcomers to start selling, in an industry where it's established that becoming productive as a sales person takes time.
- When the company's offerings are complex.

The company needs to decide the length of the draw (typically six to twelve months). This depends on:

- Sales cycle length
- Payment frequency
- Affordability of the draw

- Time needed for the sales person to become productive

Draws can be recoverable (when the sales person needs to give back the draw from the money he earns as commission) or non-recoverable (sales person keeps it all regardless of their performance).

Local Factors

If a company has a nationwide or especially a global sales force, it's important to take into account local factors that affect each local sales team. These include:

- Societal custom and trends (for example, is this an area where a group is more important than the individual performance, or one where relationships with clients is considered more important than sales).

- Market structures, maturity and business objectives (for example, in some markets one needs to work together with government agencies or other partners).

- Embedded employment practices (for example how the country or area in question treats its employees in law and what benefits and perks are given).

- Legal requirements (for example local employment law and whether there is any specific requirement as to how to treat incentives).

Understanding local factors is vital as in some cases they might necessitate having a different sales crediting scheme for sales people in different areas.

Central vs Local Decision Making

In many cases a sales opportunity involves stakeholders in more than one country. In a case like this local management and central offices might both be involved. Buying processes might be dictated from the headquarters. It can quickly become complex.

In cases like this, there is often more than one sales person involved. For example, there might be one sales person dealing with the territory near HQ, while other deals with the local subsidiary in another country. It's important to decide exactly how these two should work together, what each one is responsible for, and who gets credit when a sale is closed.

Questions To Answer To Help With Central vs Local Policies

When deciding how to treat sales for a multinational company, management needs to consider:

- How many people are involved and at which level?
- Is it better to split the commission (credit split) or pay all parties differently (multiple credit)?
- Who is leading the sale, who is putting in most effort and who is secondary in the effort?
- What type of sales roles are involved? Key Account Managers, local sales?
- Is there a lead from HQ or a lead from local market?
- If there is a local decision, is the local market working with a preferred list of providers from HQ?

Let's look at two examples of how to analyse this.

The first example is a company that buys centrally, then distributes to local entities. In this case, they need to answer:

- Where is the need coming from, locally or imposed by the HQ?
- Can local needs take priority?

The second example is a company that lets regional and local entities buy independently. This company needs to consider:

- Is there involvement and decision process in HQ?
- Are there any factors imposed by HQ?
- Does the vendor need to muscle anyone in the HQ?

Taking the time to answer these questions now saves a company from stress and tension between HQ and regional and global offices further down the road.

Incentivizing The Sales Manager

The final specific item to consider is how to incentivize the sales manager. For a company to be effective, the whole sales force needs to be aligned. That includes sales managers.

Most organisations have a sales team headed by a manager. The teams might be split up according to several factors, such as:

- Products
- Vertical industries
- Horizontal product teams
- Regional teams
- Key account teams

The sales manager shares the objectives of their sales team members, but also has other objectives beyond those of the sales people.

To properly decide how to build an incentives scheme for a sales manager, you need to start with a thorough examination of their role, objectives, responsibilities and day to day tasks. Having all this set down in detail makes it much easier to build an incentives scheme for them.

The Sales Manager Has A Different Role To A Sales Person's

Understanding that the role of a sales manager is different to that of a sales person is key to figuring out how best to incentivize that role.

The role of the sales manager is to manage their own sales team, rather than managing individual clients. Some of their main responsibilities include:

- Managing sales people;
- Bringing new ideas to the team and company;

149

- Helping their sales people reach their targets;
- Navigating internal tensions and negotiations between different staff members and teams;
- Helping their sales team to advance opportunities and turn them into sales; and
- Educating, coaching and encouraging their sales team to make sure they give their best performance.

Because this role is different to simply bringing sales, the incentives scheme needs to be different too. Too many companies make the mistake of thinking that the sales manager's target is essentially all his individual team members' targets added up. Approaching it this way doesn't encourage managers to do their best work.

Say for example a sales manager needs to work on increasing the number of team members who reach their targets, and getting more of them above a set threshold. This might be set out as:

- Their target is to have at least x percent of sales people reaching a hundred percent of their targets, or;
- Their target is to be sure that none of their sales team reach less than fifty percent of their targets.

As well as these goals, the manager might have other strategic goals too such as:

- Landing at least one big opportunity for his team in a set period.
- Selling a new contract in an untouched territory.

In addition to that he is also responsible for making sure his team stays competitive and works well as a team. To that end they also have a team achievement target to reach.

If that wasn't enough, sales managers are also responsible for:

- Making sure clients are respected.
- Ensuring their team only sells in an ethical way.

- Keeping the administration of the team running smoothly.
- Overseeing overall operation tactics.

When you see the tasks laid out like this, it's clear that trying to motivate managers based solely on sales targets is ineffective, and time must be dedicated to designing an incentives scheme that makes sense for their role.

Designing a sales incentives scheme effectively takes time and effort. Putting in the time to plan for each of these specific items helps head off any potential problems and makes sure everyone knows what to expect no matter what the day to day life of the business throws at them.

Sales Crediting; Who Will Take Credit For A Sales. One Of The Most Controversial Areas To Deal With

A sales motivation scheme is a powerful managerial tool that is used to motivate sales people to meet and exceed targets.

In order to succeed, a sales motivation scheme needs to exist alongside a good product, a competitive offering, and effective sales procedures and tools. When used properly, in both matured sales environments and in small start-ups, it can help revenues exceed targets and expectations.

The motivation scheme has many variables that need to be clarified and lots of processes to be followed. It is not just a simple decision what percentage the system should pay or whether there will be a cap to the scheme.

One of the most important things to clarify is who, when, and how to credit sales. In this article we're going to take a deep dive into this topic so you can ensure your sales crediting procedures are the most effective possible.

Who Deserves The Sales Credit?

One of the challenging matters and one of the first to tackle when designing a sales motivation scheme is the idea of sales crediting.

At first glance this sounds simple. You make a sale; you get the credit – right? But in practice it's rarely that simple. Does one single person (the one who signs the final deal) get all the credit? Or does it get split between a team of people who worked on the deal?

Every company needs to take into careful consideration which factors and elements to consider when giving credit for sales. Some of the key factors to consider include:

- Who is the owner of the opportunity?
- How much effort did each specific person put into the closing process?
- What are each interested person's relations with the main stakeholders?
- Where was the contract signed?

- Whose budget supports the opportunity?
- Who has the traditional account relation with the company the sale was made to?

It Usually Takes More Than One Person To Close An Opportunity

As you can see from the above paragraph, *it's not at all unusual for more than one person to be involved in closing a sales opportunity.* Quite often, employees who are not even necessarily from the sales department play a vital part in the sales process. This is especially true when selling to a strategic or a global account. If a customer has offices in more than one location, both regional sales people and global account managers take part in the sales process.

Complex offerings also involve more than one sales person. Some packaged solutions are so complicated that an army of support staff help the sales person close the deal.

On top of that, companies use additional sales channels such as inside sales and marketing teams whose primary role is to find and qualify leads before the sales force even sees that lead. Pre sales people and sales specialists are also working next to the sales person to provide technical knowledge and expertise. There are organisations where the sales people are responsible for everything along the sales cycle whereas in other cases the sales person starts working with a client only when there is a well-qualified opportunity.

The Question Is How To Credit The Sale

Who is carrying the quota, who is responsible for leading the sales effort on the deal, and who is credited for the eventual sale?

Most importantly of all: Who gets the commission?

These are not easy questions to answer. To properly fulfil its function, the sales scheme needs to keep all staff motivated, who are involved in a sale. Everyone involved should feel that they will be recognised somehow for their effort and they must feel they are an important part of the team.

After all, if the inside sales team didn't qualify the leads, there would be no warm leads. If the specialist didn't provide a perfect system demo, there'd be much less chance of proceeding to a sale.

In all of the above challenges there are various ways and answers and the company must consider all alternatives before deciding and communicating how to handle those difficult sales cases.

Start By Analysing The Opportunity Lifecycle

Analysing the opportunity lifecycle is an excellent way to get a feel for how many people are involved in a sale.

Say for example an inside sales person arranges a few cold calls and is able to find an opportunity with a new client that has no existing relation with the company.

The opportunity after the qualification stage is given to the sales manager who is responsible for engaging with the client, presenting the value proposition and closing the deal. A sales specialist who doesn't carry a quota is also assigned from the relevant product team to help the sales manager secure the deal.

To make it more complicated imagine that we also have a strategic account manager who has the overall responsibility of managing the account but allows other sales people that represent different products to step in and sell.

So far, four people have been involved in the sale:

- The sales person who made the cold call;
- The sales manager who engages with the client;
- The sales specialist who helps secure the deal; and
- The strategic account manager.

Some cases even involve external channels. For example, a redistributor in the retail market is someone that stands between the factory and the final consumer. She might not share the same commission with the sales person but their profit affects the margin of the product as it is consumed before reaching the end client.

Having Rules In Place Is Vital

As part of the sales motivation guidelines and procedures, every company needs to have certain rules governing how credit is assigned and how commissions are paid in all possible scenarios.

Depending on the nature of the business, different rules might apply in different circumstances. For example, in some cases one commission might be split between the people involved, where in others, extra commissions might be paid to reward more than one person involved in the process.

Even if a certain guideline is not always followed, there needs to be an objective way to decide each how the commissions are split. Let's not forget that for sales people their commission is perhaps the most vital element in their job and they need to know in advance the financial outcome of any sales opportunity they are working on.

Two Examples Of How Sales Could Be Credited In Different Scenarios

To better understand how sales credit might be split between different people, let's look at two scenarios.

Scenario one. A sales opportunity exists within an IT company that sells multi million solutions. The people involved include:

- A strategic account manager managing the relation with this account.
- A sales person dedicated to the certain product that is offered in this opportunity.
- A technical specialist.

The strategic account manager found the opportunity. He's also responsible for all commercial negotiation. He influenced the client and added the terms together to close the deal.

The product sales person drove fifty percent of the opportunity as he had to give inside information, build the case, etc.

The technical specialist presents and demonstrates the product to the client.

In this case, all three people get awarded. If the incentives opportunity for this deal is for example $10,000 then we could offer both the product and the strategic sales person the full commission of $10,000 each. That means the company is paying 2x the incentive.

However, both could give up ten percent of their commission to the technical specialist, as their role was also vital.

If the scenario was slightly different and the opportunity was found by the product sales person, but the strategic account manager's job was to secure the deal through his strong relations with the client, the latter could earn thirty percent of the incentives opportunity as this should work as a referral commission.

Scenario two. A sales person is working on an opportunity that came from an inbound call after a strong marketing campaign.

The opportunity came about because of the efforts of a pre-sales team that worked massively into the requirements list and the technical documents. The sales person talks about the added value but the pre-sales team actually "shows" it.

In this case unless the pre-sales team is under a separate motivation scheme, they need to get credit.

Anyone that works in an opportunity either directly by talking to the client or indirectly by providing information to the sales person, needs some motivation to keep adding value to the sales process. Otherwise they won't put in as much effort and the company will suffer.

In this particular case two distinctive commission plans should be in place. And the incentives opportunity given to both people should be 1.5 x of the incentives opportunity of the deal.

What These Scenarios Teach Us About Sales Crediting

Analysing these two scenarios teaches us two things about sales crediting.

First, that there are three main categories of who gets credit for a sale:

1. **Sales people** – if as per above examples more than one person is involved in making a sale, the credit can be split.

2. **Vertical** – management may get a cut of the sales, such as the manager of the sales person above.

3. **Horizontal** - others that helped such as the technical specialist in scenario one and the pre sales team in scenario two.

What a company needs to consider is the total cost of incentives and not the individual one. If one sums up the individual incentives given in a deal then it may eat a lot of the profit margin.

The second thing we can learn from this is that there are, broadly speaking, three criteria that make someone eligible for sales credit:

- They influenced the decision of the client

- They moved an opportunity to a next stage

- They had direct customer relations

Getting this right is vital – sales people need to be motivated or the whole thing will come crashing down. One key element of this is timing when to pay commissions. Let's take a closer look at timing.

Deciding When To Pay Sales Commission

Often referred to as "persuasion", the goal in sales is to offer prospective clients solutions to make their lives easier and simpler, and thus to create a win-win-win scenario for the sales person, the company and the customer.

The goal of a sales compensation plan is to persuade the sales team to sell the right products to the right clients. This requires the right incentives at the right time within the sales process to keep the sales person happy financially.

Depending on the industry, the product, the sales process and supporting functions, the level of persuasion needed can be different. For example, in the case of a supermarket or an online store a sales person has almost no involvement in persuading a customer. This work is done through efficient marketing campaigns.

However, in a complex deal where many people are involved in selling a software solution to a big global organisation, the role of a sales person is to create a series of winning decisions. Through negotiations with people in many different departments, and by reaching successful outcomes, sales people are financially rewarded.

In situations like this, deciding when to pay sales commissions is vitally important.

Three Key Factors To Consider In Deciding When To Pay Sales Commission

Deciding **when** to gives sales credit is important. The four main options are:

- Receipt of order
- Signature of agreement
- Implementation
- Customer payment

The question is, how do you determine which is the right point in the process to award credits to a sales person?

There's no "one size fits all" answer to this question, as situations and circumstances vary, and cannot be generalized. However, here are three factors to consider:

Company strategy

A startup company has totally different short-term objectives than a company that has been operating for twenty years in the market.

The startup might be looking to approach a very specific industry and get known, whereas a matured business might need to retain the best customers they have.

Each compensation scheme would reflect the company's strategies and short and long term goals.

Market convention

"That's what everybody does in this industry" doesn't always work. Often companies stand out in the market place because they have broken market conventions.

Although this is a personal decision, it does depend what others in your industry are doing and what the current situation in the market is.

For example, in a deep crisis period, the objectives of the company may change to prioritizing the retention of the customers. Compensation schemes that were geared towards obtaining new clients may need to be revised to encourage the sales team to focus much more on upselling or cross selling to existing clients. This strategy allows the company to increase its revenue stream from their regular clients.

In these cases, the point at which the sales people are compensated might be adjusted to suit the market conditions.

Sales force maturity

Is a sales person capable and skilled sufficiently to drive the whole process from creating interest to fulfilling the order? Do they put in the majority of the effort needed to close the sale and keep the customer happy? Or are they newer and needing more support?

Depending on the experience and the maturity of the sales force, the company might incentivize them differently.

Risks To Keep In Mind In Deciding When To Pay Commission

In any part of running a business, you should always consider the potential risks. When it comes to deciding when to pay sales commission, you need to consider:

The legal aspects

Often the process of sorting out all the legal aspects involved in the deal can take up as much time as the selling and having the client accepting an offer. So, keep in mind how long this part will take.

When a sale is considered to fall over

If the salesperson puts in time and effort to complete a sale, only to have the lawyers step in and pull the rug from under the sale, should the sales person still be compensated? Should a sales credit be given with the acceptance of the offer from a client or with the signature of the agreement?

What happens in the case of early settlement?

What happens if a customer is approved a bank loan, and the bank officer receives his commission, right after a loan is disbursed to a customer? The next day the customer repays the total outstanding loan, without earning interest for the bank. Should the whole payment of commissions take place straight after the sale or wait for the action of customers?

Sales performance

A sales person is paid based on their performance, typically assessed by annual or monthly sales targets set by the management team. Most of these targets are quantifiable and measured in financial or other incentives. For example, a car sales person is expected to sell a minimum number each month, with a target of units to sell by the end of the year. In other cases sales people have targets in terms of profit they make or value the products sold worth. It's important to consider how sales proficiency intersect with the timing of paying sales commissions.

What happens if an order is cancelled?

Every company needs a policy that deals with returns and cancellations. How shall the company act when incentives have already been paid in these cases? Perhaps incentives shall be paid after the cancellation and refund window is lapsed.

What happens if a customer doesn't pay?

If a customer doesn't pay and is delinquent shall the sales person get penalised and not having his incentives paid? This is something the company must consider (hint: Most sales people will not take kindly to be punished for a customer's bad behaviour).

What about other situations where payment might be delayed?

What if installation is delayed by years? And what if this delay is due to the client's failure to allocate the right resources to the project? Or what if the company promised to deliver something that they cannot deliver and the client sues the company? It's important to know what happens in all these circumstances that create risk around the sales process.

The Risks Of Paying Too Early Or Too Late

There are risks involved in paying too soon, or not soon enough.

By paying a sales commission before the sale is completed, the company runs the risk that the sales person will believe their work to be done, and move on to their next opportunity for financial renumeration.

On the other hand, if they pay commission too late in the sales process, the company runs the risk that the sales person will lose motivation, and become demoralized. In that instance too, they might abandon the sales process to focus on their next opportunity for financial renumeration. They might also look for opportunities with other companies offering more favourable compensation schemes.

Say for example a company sells a large computer system and pays commission after the system is successfully implemented at the client's site. After the sales person's work is done, they have to wait for technical support to drive the installation to the final stage to complete the sale. Now they no longer have any input or control in the process, but are paid only at the time where the agreement is signed from the customer. How would the sales person feel if they had to wait for two years before the installation is completed?

Or what if the installation is never done? This results in negative consequences of reputation risk and legal risk for the company.

A close friend of mine working in the banking sector once told me that a system they bought many years ago was never installed during the ten-year term of the agreement. Although the client paid, there were disputes about some payments, and the software company's reputation was adversely affected. Although in this particular case, the commission was paid to the sales person, it illustrates the dangers of waiting till a system is installed.

Deciding When To Pay Sales Credit – A Working Example

Let's look at an example to help us consider all the aspects that feed into the decision. **When is a sale deemed to be finalized, and at what stage of completion of the sale does the sales agent get paid their commission?**

Not every sales transaction is a simple process of handing over money in exchange for the supply of goods or services such as would be found at a car boot sale. Take, for instance, real estate or other negotiations where the final transaction follows a series of successful stages, that could take months, or even years, to finalize.

Let's imagine a team member named Kyle. Kyle works for many months at negotiating an intricate contract, resolving a number of factors, to arrive at a complex solution that:

- Costs a couple of millions of dollars to the client,
- Includes licenses for five years,
- Requires various phases of development and implementation,
- Has a service agreement where the customer pays for annual support and maintenance costs.
- The product/service may take up to one year to install;
- Requires a team of three people to work on the implementation; and
- Is paid for with split invoices
- to different locations
- in different periods and
- according to usage of the solution and
- the number of users.

All the above factors create a dilemma of how to structure the sales commissions and incentives for such a complex sale. To be fair to both the company and to Kyle, answers need to be found to such questions as:

- When is the right time to pay commissions for this sale?

- When is sales credit given to the sales person?

- When is the deal determined to have been completed?

- The documents have been signed, or

- The contract has been implemented, or

- When invoices are paid?

These questions open up another can of worms. The concern for the Kyle is how the company determines at which point in the sales cycle will Kyle see his commission?

When Should Kyle Be Paid?

The answer to the above question is not straightforward as you may think. There are now a number of factors in the equation:

- The mindset of the organisation and its culture.

- The size of the organisation, and its accounting principles.

- The culture of the sales force.

- The objectives of management.

- The nature of the products.

- Current acceptable market practice (how do other companies handle it).

In addition, the company must consider risk factors such as:

- What happens if the sale is delayed?

- How those delays affect the sales contract.

- Whether the commitment from the company to deliver is or is not meeting the SLAs (service level agreement) signed.

We can analyse the issue here from two different perspectives, with both approaches presenting a solution:

- From the company's viewpoint. At what point of the timeline does the accounting department record the transaction as a sale?
- Unless the commission payment is seen as an advance of commission due, then for a sales credit to be issued, a sale has to be first accounted for in the company's books.
- So, for example, according to the accounting standards the company chooses to follow, it needs to record the sale. And once the invoice is issued, the company might use this point in the timeline of the sales process to release the sales credit to the salesperson.
- From Kyle's viewpoint. In general, there are no strict rules that enforce a company to follow their accounting process as relates to sales credit. Commissions can just as easily follow the sales process.
- If there is no valid reason why Kyle cannot be given a sales credit when a contract is signed with the client. Indeed, it may be that the benefits of maintaining the morale of the sales department by paying the commissions at that point are greater than the drawbacks.

Sales People Need To Eat!

Kyle is, as it happens, a real person. While catching up over a cup of coffee a few months ago, Kyle told me about his frustration with his sales position for an IT company, and in particular with the way sales credit was given.

Since only a portion of his commissions were credited and paid upon invoicing the client, he was frustrated. After all, securing the deal was the only part of the whole transaction that Kyle had a hands-on involvement with.

He was frustrated with having to wait for other people in the company to carry out the installation of the system, before he could receive the second part of his commission payment. He justifiably felt it unfair, since that part of the sales process had nothing to do with his role and or his skills as a sales person. Being at the mercy of other departments while he waited for his payment was not helping his performance.

Kyle's situation highlights a third factor that needs to be taken into account when deciding which approach to follow.

Wrong Timing Is A Quick Track To A Demotivated Sales Force

If the company is not careful to fully consider the sales process from invoicing through to completion of the product or service being supplied, they run the risk of a very demotivated sales force.

From Kyle's perspective, his job is done once the paperwork has been signed and the contract has been invoiced. And it is Kyle's best interest to get his commissions as soon as he can.

It only seems fair that once their job is done, and the sales agents have earned their sales commissions, their payments should be released accordingly.

One way to avoid such conflict between management and staff, is for the sales management to have clear agreements in place. These agreements must include:

- The roles and responsibilities of the sales people.
- A clear layout of the sales process.
- At what stage in the process they will receive their commissions.

By explaining what they require from their sales team at the outset, a company can better avoid misunderstandings down the track.

Let's have another look at Kyle, in his role as a product sales specialist, and Jeremy, who is a key account manager working with Kyle, selling IT systems.

If Kyle gets the sales credit when the agreement is signed, then Jeremy, the key account manager, may have to ensure the implementation of the system is smooth, so the sales credit comes at a later stage.

In this example, you can see how vital it is for a sales person like Kyle, to have a clear understanding of his role and responsibilities in the sales process, and help eliminate any feelings of frustration or being demoralized.

Remember, an incentives plan is a management tool that exists to motivate sales people, and careful consideration of the policy behind sales credits can eliminate problems that could arise in the future.

When sales people believe they deserve to get their sales credit earlier, and then don't get them, it creates discontent, which can cause not only demotivation but damage to the reputation of the company.

Points To Consider When Deciding On The Timing Of Sales Credit

We've seen how Kyle became demoralized through misunderstanding. Let's look at other factors to consider in policy making and designing motivation schemes.

By overlooking the timing of sales credits there's a big risk of creating a frustrated sales team. People might think that there is an obvious answer to this question. Sales commissions must be paid when the customer signs the contract. This is quite common but not the only case.

There are other important aspects to consider when deciding when to pay, such as:

Whether the company is especially focused on building a relationship with a client. In this case, they might reward the sales people before any contracts are signed with the customer, in anticipation of a future sale. Here there is a risk that a contract is never signed by the client.

The guidance of the finance team. What do they say about how the company records the revenues into its accounting books? The interest of the finance department is to tie together the revenue booking and the incentives, on a timeline. This includes when the order is booked into the accounting system, when the invoice is issued, and when the customer pays the invoice. During any financial year the finance department might be dealing with multiple invoices that are issued and paid in different times.

How the product adds or detracts from revenues that are landing in the company. One must always consider things from the product side, and its effect on the profit or loss for the company, in terms of quantities and cost of goods sold.

Smooth implementation and delivery of the service to the client. A slow or delayed implementation is not good for the reputation of the company; it will worsen the relation between the client and the company. One must consider both the implementation schedule and the timeframe for delivery and installation.

Questions To Ask To Help Make The Decision On When To Pay

All the above aspects are important when it comes to deciding when to pay commission, but how, in the end, should a company actually decide when to pay?

There are two ways to approach this: One that focuses on benefitting the company (paying when the entire deal is complete including installation), and one that focuses on benefitting the sales person (paying before installation is complete.)

In my opinion it is important to look after the sales person, for without their effort and skill, the company will struggle. So, the responsibility rests with the company to define the sales role and responsibilities in a way that both fits with management objectives and motivates the sales force.

These questions provide a good starting point for discussion when deciding the best time to pay sales credits:

- What is current market practice in our industry?
- What is the sales role and the responsibilities of the sales person? Is it:
- To have the agreement signed?
- To have the agreement signed and then drive the implementation?
- To make the client pay upon receipt of invoice?
- What is the objective of the company in regards to the motivation scheme? Is it:
- To retain good sales people?
- To make sales people responsible for additional tasks?
- What is the objective of the company? Is it:
- To bring new clients?
- To make existing clients happy?
- What is the nature of business and the project value? Does it prioritize:
- Big volume tickets, or
- Low volume but big value tickets?

- By answering the above questions, policy makers can make an informed decision about the best time to give sales credit and pay commissions.

If for example it is clear that a sales person's responsibility is solely to have the client sign the agreement, then all sales credit shall be released at the time of signing.

If on the other hand, the company feels that customer retention is a priority, and the optimum objective is to keep clients happy, then sales credit could be given at the end of the sale, once the product is delivered, and the client has paid and is happy.

An alternative answer to the problem that I personally support, is to split the commission into different portions to be paid at specific milestones of the sale. For example, one can give fifty percent sales credit when the agreement is signed and another fifty percent when installation is done.

In any event, the timing of sales credits should always reflect the responsibilities and the role of the sales person.

Always Keep Policy Documents

It is important to have a policy document that covers the handling of specific, often common, problems such as:

- Refunds
- Cancellations
- Non payment
- Disputes

For instance, let's say that all sales credit is given when the customer signs the agreement. There is always the risk the client doesn't pay the invoice that is issued straight after, and he can pay within thirty days. The company can give sales credit seventy percent upon signature and the remaining thirty percent after ninety days, provided the customer pays.

If you have a policy document that covers all such instances, your team will know how to handle them should they arise, and your salespeople will know what to expect.

For example, in our above scenario, the policy document could set out that it's the sales person's responsibility to follow up the payment of the invoices, and secure their remaining commission payment.

As with everything, communication in the sales division is important for all parties, and by having established guidelines everybody's job can be made so much easier.

Is There A Place For Out-Of-Policy Sales Credits?

I spent part of my career at a financial institution, designing commission plans for a sales force of more than a thousand people. The sales reports soon flagged up the fact that some people were low performing when it came to sales. It didn't seem that unusual at first – in a sales force of that size, some people are always going to underperform.

But there was something strange about this case.

All the underperforming people had previously done well and had established reputations as being great sales people.

So why the sudden change in achievement?

I took a closer look at the reports, and the answer became clear: Our salespeople had to achieve at least sixty percent success rate in all of their three measures (targets) in order to get a commission payout. That meant they could have an outstanding performance of a hundred percent in two targets, but if the third was at fifty eight percent they'd get nothing.

I had to wonder if the system was too rigid. Would our sales people really be motivated to do their best work, knowing that no matter how well they did, missing just one out of three targets by a couple of percent meant they got nothing for their efforts?

I'm giving you this example because it illustrates the final point I want to make while we're talking about sales crediting: That in some cases there is a place for out-of-policy sales credits.

The Case For Out-Of-Policy Payments

In cases like the one I just outlined, where a salesperson has performed well or contributed significantly to their employer, but still doesn't see a payout, there is a risk of:

- **High turnover of sales people.** Constantly missing commissions despite performing well is frustrating, and the sales person might well leave for a company that offers a better system. Not every system suits every sales person, but if there is a pattern emerging, it's time to look at an exemption system for out-of-policy payments.

- **Low performance.** Think about the salespeople at my old financial employer. No one could blame them for getting so frustrated that they stopped trying as hard – and that would be bad for both the sales person and the team.

- **Other objectives not being met.** If a sales person has other duties, such as creating a new market or penetrating a strategic account, he wants to know he will still be fairly compensated for his efforts. If he's only being paid commission for direct sales, he won't give as much attention to the other objectives.

When Out-Of-Policy Sales Credits Are Useful

Imagine for a moment that a tech startup is struggling to get established due to well-known competitors who are backed by an experienced sales force and a strong brand reputation. After a year of trying to break into the market, one of the sales team lands a huge client, one who could change everything. Yet because the initial sale doesn't quite reach the commission threshold, they still get nothing for the effort.

In cases like this, management might decide that a payment outside the commission plan is in order. After all, the new client is potentially worth a huge amount to the company, and the salesperson might have just turned the company's fortunes around. It would be a shame if they then left because the system doesn't allow them to be compensated for that effort – plus they might spread the word and damage the company's reputation.

Out-of-policy sales credits could be deemed appropriate for:

- A sale that wasn't forecasted, but that makes a big difference to the company.
- A significant sale that ushers in a new era or turns the company's fortunes around.
- A notable sale that management wants to reward as an example to the rest of the sales force.
- Two people work together and though their individual results are under target, as a team they've brought in a significant amount of sales.
- Events such as significant client acquisition, cross selling, or anything else that isn't covered by the commission system but is a notable achievement.
- Any situation where commission guidelines have not been met, but where managers believe a payment would be appropriate.

Change The System Or Make An Exception?

There are two potential ways to handle situations like those I've outlined here: Management can either change the system to cover such situations, or treat specific events as exemptions.

If there's a noticeable trend of good sales people falling through the cracks and not getting commissions, or sales staff turnover is on the rise, it might be time to consider changing the system.

On the other hand, if the system is working fine but there are simply a few notable exceptions, treating them as an exemption will be easier and more cost effective than changing the whole system.

In my opinion, the latter is the best option in all but a rare few cases. It's impossible to come up with a system that covers all cases and events, which makes it difficult to draw up a totally comprehensive policy. It's simply more practical to make exemptions.

Out-Of-Policy Payments Must Be Carefully Planned

There may be cases where an exemption is the best choice, but it's important to keep in mind that out-of-policy payments can still be high risk for a company, both financially and in terms of operations. That's why I recommend a company takes the following steps:

Set up an exemption committee. Imagine the consequences if the power to approve exemptions was given to the wrong person: Unfair decisions, too many or not enough exemptions, an uneven policy and a disgruntled sales force.

Set up an exemption committee to make decisions together. I recommend having one team to carry out the preliminary assessment and make recommendations, and a senior management team to assess their findings and make the final decision on payment.

Write up an exemption policy. Even though each case will need to be assessed individually, there will still be rules and regulations. You should include topics such as:

- Who can approve exemptions?
- What does the approval process look like?
- What is each person on the committee responsible for?
- How long do decisions take and how are they communicated?
- How is the payment amount decided upon?
- How and when are payments made?

Be clear about approving lines. Part of the policy must include a very clear understanding of who has the power to approve what.

Start a log book. Keep a record of:

- How many exemptions are given?

- How much was paid
- Who they were given to?
- Who approved them?

Audit regularly. The log book should be audited every six months to ensure that exemptions are being allocated fairly. If one person seems to be getting a lot of exemptions, it's important to know they were given with good will and no favouritism is being shown.

Auditing also flags up potential problems with both the exemption system and the commission system. For example, if a company finds too many exemptions are being given for extraordinary items, there's a real risk that the extraordinary items will become ordinary and the company will end up paying too much out of pocket. Auditing lets companies see where policies are faulty and need to be rewritten.

No sales commission structure can cover every possible scenario. A robust exemption policy lets a business reward sales people for exceptional work that falls outside of the policy.

Deciding on how and when to give sales credit takes time and focus, and is worth spending time and energy on. A good sales credit policy (that also allows for exceptions) is a major component in keeping your sales force motivated and productive. Next time you are asked to design a sales incentives scheme or commission plan, go through the points in this article first. That way you'll reduce the risk of losing your top sales performers, by ensuring you carefully consider the right time to award sales credits to your sales team.

Quota Distribution. Why Assigning Targets Is So Crucial And Why It Leads To The Failure Of The System

Every time the end of the financial year rolls around, budget discussions become commonplace. The sales for the current year are almost done, and sales people are in a hurry to close opportunities in their pipeline. Everyone expects to have bigger targets for the next year.

Targets (interchangeably called quotas) are the standard by which sales people are appraised. How much of the target a sales person achieves is part of any appraisal, and knowing targets gives sales people a clear idea of how much money they can reasonably expect to make.

Why Targets Are The Most Important Part Of A Sales Incentives Plan

Targets are arguably the most important part of any sales incentives plan. Targets control how much a sales person can get paid, in both the fixed and variable parts of the scheme.

Let's look at an example.

Charles has a fair target of $100,000. He gets five percent for sales up to fifty percent of target, seven percent from $50,000 to $100,000 and eleven percent for anything above $100,000.

If Charles sells products worth $150,000 he will pocket (50,000 x 5%) + (50,000 x 7%) + (50,000 x 11%) = 2,500+3,500+5,500=$11,500

Now imagine the target was set wrongly to $200,000 and he still made $150,000 of revenues. Using the same commission levels as before Charles would pocket (100,000 x 5%) + (50,000 x 7%) = 5,000+3,500 = $8,500 which is a significant difference in pocketed money from the first amount.

The target directly determines the payout a sales person can get, and therefore it directly influences his motivation. How motivated a sales person is directly affects how much money a company can make.

The Consequences Of Incorrectly Set Targets

A couple of years back a startup approached us for help with their incentives scheme. They had three sales people, and none of them were very motivated. We noticed straight away that the target for each person was at least $750,000 in a year. However, the product was a complex one with a sales cycle of more than a year, so no one expected to make commissions, and thus, had no motivation. We suggested splitting the incentives into two and incentivizing smaller sales too.

As you can see, wrongly set targets can have serious consequences. We recently surveyed our clients and found that setting targets was one of the top problematic areas for all of them. In addition, they told us some of the consequences they've found when their targets are set incorrectly:

- **Sales people think they can't reach the target, so they stop trying as hard**. Sales people are competitive by nature – reaching their targets is an ongoing competition with themselves, and with others. Sales people want to be the highest achievers and rank well. Targets that make it hard to do so are demotivating.

- **Sales people turn to unethical tactics**. In some cases, a sales person might choose more unethical tactics to reach difficult targets, such as selling products and services a client doesn't really need, or finding a way to inflate prices.

- **Sales people think the next year might be better, so they purposely leave some contracts until the next sales period, so they can reach their target in that period**.

- **Wrongly set targets lead to frustrated sales people, who then leave the company**. Seeing that a target is too high to be fairly achievable is one of the leading reasons that sales people leave their firms.

- **Unmotivated sales people and / or high sales turnover directly impacts the company's revenues**.

Not All Targets Are Measured In Individual Sales

Before we go any further, it's important to understand that not all targets are measured in individual sales. For example, a target might be to bring $1 million of new revenues, or it might be to bring three new clients, or to increase customer satisfaction by fifteen percent. It might be to penetrate a specific new market.

Every company has its own goals, and those goals change every single sales period. Perhaps today the goal is to penetrate into a new industry, and next year it's to advance sales. The target right now might be to sell two new contracts to a new industry in a new country, while the next year it's specifically to sell $200,000 worth in that country.

Quotas might be set in:

- Units sold

- Monetary values

- Via a points system (each point is worth certain $ and each product sale is worth different points)

Indicators That A Company's Issues Are Related To Target Setting

I once heard the head of sales in a huge company say he had a dream that in the following year all sales people would reach their targets. In theory this sounds good. However, in the real world, every person meeting their targets is actually a sign the targets were not set correctly. Ideally, you want seventy to eighty percent of sales people to reach their targets. If everyone is hitting their targets, the targets are too low. Here are some more indicators that incorrect targets are causing problems:

The target doesn't match the aims. As we just discussed, not every target is directly sales related. If a company is focussed on acquiring a new target audience, but the sales team is working on gaining revenues from existing customers there's a mismatch.

The sales force is reaching their targets, but incentives payments are bigger or smaller than expected. If targets are being met, but payments are significantly bigger or smaller than the target incentives, there could be an unequal target allocation.

Too many people are reaching the sales cap. If you've set a cap but too many people are reaching it, either the cap is wrong, or the sales targets are wrong.

Sales people have very different target performance than others in their team. There's bound to be some variation in performance, but if there's a big disparity or some people are performing either very randomly, or continuously underperforming, there could be a problem.

Three Ways To Set Targets

Now we know why targets are so important, and how incorrectly setting them can lead to problems. The next thing to do is figure out how to set them.

It's important to realise that targets are not an arbitrary number. I recently spoke with the head of sales in a tech company. We quickly identified that he was setting targets arbitrarily. He took the number his CEO gave him and split it equally between their sales team of eight. There was no methodology behind it. As a result, some sales people were overperforming by over two hundred percent, while some were performing at less than seventy percent.

Instead of this scattergun approach, let's look at some tried and tested ways to set sales targets.

The Top to Bottom Approach

The top to bottom approach starts with management deciding on key objectives. This decision is usually decided between departments and is based on objectives and goals that are directly related to increasing profitability. These goals are then translated into quantifiable targets for the sales team. For example, a company might decide their aim is to bring $10 million of new revenues in the next year, based on the previous year's numbers adjusted for factors such as:

- Market conditions
- Competition this year
- Sales force capabilities, skills and turnover
- Product suite offered next period
- Dynamics of the company and how efficient sales are

When to use this approach

This approach is data and history-driven, and is well suited to mature businesses with a commercial approach. Use this when there is a central board of directors in charge, and a large sales force.

The Bottom Up Approach

This approach starts with the sales team. Sales are predicted according to sales capabilities, territories, and historical performance. The sales team then negotiate with management to agree their targets. Each sales person assesses their territory, their history, and their dynamic, and also lends their expertise regarding the campaigns they'll need to run to reach their targets.

When to use this approach

This approach works best in medium sized organisations where sales people have a clear idea of the market conditions and potential. It relies on sales people having worked in their roles long enough to have in-depth knowledge of their regions and potential.

The Combined Approach

I've found that for many companies a combination of these methodologies is the best approach. The management gives a number to reach and a clear direction of what the company expects. The sales people work on their own targets, and then the two are compared and a compromise reached. Of course, management will try to stretch the targets up and sales people will try to bring them down a little, but if they can meet in the middle, they can create a target that works for sales people and keeps management happy too.

When to use this approach

This approach works well for small companies where both management and sales people feel an equal responsibility to bring in more business. It also works well in situations where sales management rely on, and are happy to rely on, the feedback and involvement of their sales team.

The Main Factors To Consider When Setting Targets

There are lots of factors to consider when setting targets. The main ones are:

Current book of business. This is the base which will determine the next period's targets because most of the new sales are predicted to come from existing clients in many product areas.

Previous year's results. This isn't just the previous year, but the history of many years back. This shows the trend and growth in revenues and helps predict future trends.

Sales roles and products sold. This along with the effort and ticket sizes and the number of deals done per year can show the trends year on year. The target must be feasible considering past average ticket sizes and sales volumes.

Territory analysis and potential. How is a territory performing throughout the year? The analysis of a region on its macroeconomic profile plays a significant role in setting targets. Are there dissimilarities between different regions? These will affect the targets for each region. One needs to quantify not only the existing business but also the future potential of a territory or an industry. How is a territory likely to develop in the future? Is the political situation stable and does it nurture growth and development?

Product development and fit to a specific target audience. One needs to consider how the product fits into the economy of a territory and local businesses. Does it fit as it is or does it need altering to fit the specific market? Are there dissimilarities in the product between different regions and is it hard to sell to certain industries, or is it a newly launched product? What about a territory where lots of competitors are already active for a long time?

In addition to these key factors, it's also wise to consider:

Seasonality. Some products follow certain sales cycles, for example tourist goods are usually sold just before the tourist season starts, or during that period.

Market uncertainty. There are reasons that regions or industries or even whole markets can become more uncertain. For example, a financial crisis might disturb the development of a country and make future growth unpredictable. In these cases, historical market performance isn't a good indicator of future trends.

The impact of a long sales cycle. This is especially true of complex products that sell for millions of dollars. The sales process is not easy and may take long as long as a couple of years. In cases like this a delay in just one thing, for example budget approval, might delay a project by a year or more. In that case setting targets is tricky.

Periodic mega orders. If a company wins mega orders from time to time, it can be difficult to forecast when those might come and how they'll affect targets. My suggestion on this matter is to treat them separately. You can engineer a scheme just for them and leave them outside the target setting.

New product offerings. If a company develops a new offering, it can be hard to forecast revenues from it in the near future. One of my suggestion is to exclude new products from target setting for the first two years.

The Role Of Data In Target Setting

One surefire way to cut down some of the uncertainty and make good decisions about targets is to make the most of the available data. Whether you use a top to bottom, bottom up, or combined approach, more data is always better. Three important bits of data to use are:

- The historical performance of the company in this specific geographical region or history. This data would include past sales targets and how well sales people did over different periods.
- The demographic and economic data for each sales region and industry. If possible, this should include statistics showing the development of the country, growth and investments.
- Qualitative factors such as any challenges in the region (recession or financial crisis), the political landscape, trade sanctions, and the country's international relations.

Accurate data is a must. For example, if the historical performance of a region isn't recorded correctly, then the data might show greater success than the sales people actually achieved. Management then set higher targets, which are hard to reach, and the sales team becomes demoralised. Good, clear, accurate data is invaluable in setting targets.

Three Key Characteristics Of Quotas

In light of all the above factors, it's important that the final quotas meet all three of these characteristics:

- They're fair. Territories are different and have different potentials. Selling in a promising and well matured market is different than selling in a new market. For example, selling $1 million of a product to an established market in Germany might take the same effort as selling $0.5 million to Portugal.

- They're realistic. Companies sometimes ask too much from sales people because they had a particularly good year previously, or they just launched a new product and they're excited about it. If targets are not realistic, sales people will stop selling because they know they can't reach them anyway.

- They're motivational. If they're too easy, sales people won't need to try hard, but if they're too hard, sales people will become unmotivated. Targets need to be just high enough that they take effort to meet, but are still achievable.

In addition to making sure they meet these three characteristics, management should take the following into account when setting quotas:

- They must be allocated in an equitable manner. By this I mean that two territories are only truly equal when they take the same amount of effort to produce the same result, and management must keep this in mind.

- They must be designed in a way that doesn't penalize the best performers. If sales management allocate more budget to the best regions, they need to make sure they're not penalizing top performers in other regions.
- They must be designed to take account of variations in territory size, potential and growth.

A Note On Whether To Tie Targets To A Person's Performance Or A Region

Whether to tie targets to a person's individual performance is a common debate in our industry.

For example, if a certain region is to produce $1 million of revenues for a specific product in the next year, should this number be increased if the sales person allocated to the task is particularly experienced and successful? Should this person have to reach $1.5 million instead?

Conversely, should management lower the target for junior sales people? Should a junior person have the same target lowered to $0.7 million?

The question comes down to this: Should targets be tied solely to the market and the region, or should it take into account personal and behavioural factors?

I believe the answer is yes, targets should be tied solely to the market. Increasing the target for more skilled people only penalizes them and makes them work harder to reach their targets than other people need to work in the same region, which breeds frustration and resentment.

Instead of changing the target based on a sales person's skill and history, it's much more effective to decide on the target for the region and then choose the sales person most likely to bring that target.

When To Adjust Quotas

As you can see there are lots of factors to take into account. As a result, quotas are a dynamic thing, and it's important to assess them regularly and adjust if necessary.

However, it's also important not to adjust them too frequently, as a client of mine learned.

I met up with Steve, the head of sales in a tech company. A good part of his sales force was not performing as standard, and he wanted help figuring out why. When we assessed the situation, it turned out that he'd adjusted the sales targets at least four times in one year. Sales people got confused and demotivated as a result, and stopped performing.

Constant assessment is important, but frequently changing targets causes confusion and leaves sales people feeling unmotivated. I've seen some companies adjust sales quotas every time they want to make more revenue, which is not a valid reason to change targets.

However, you might need to change targets during a sales period if:

- There's a major economic change in a territory.
- There's an account reshuffle.
- A sales person leaves.
- A sales person gets more territories.
- The pricing model changes.
- A territory suffers an abrupt and severe change such as a financial crisis.

To save frustration or knee-jerk reactions, I recommend all sales teams have a policy in place for what to do in all of the above scenarios.

Setting quotas is mostly a technical matter. In fact, one could even design a model considering all the factors outlined here, so the system can calculate the quotas per person.

The key to setting quotas is to collect as much information as possible about both the region and industry, and the sales team. The more demographic and economic factors you can take into account, the better the potential to forecast growth and set realistic quotas based on that.

If you take into account all the factors outlined here, you'll be able to set quotas that are fair, motivational, and clear, thus providing the impetus sales people need to reach their targets, and boost company revenues.

Territories Allocation; The Notion That Is So Well Bundled With The Incentives Scheme

The sales territory (the market a sales person covers) is another vital part of a sales compensation scheme. A sales territory tells a sales person the market they're responsible for, and gives a strong indication of the potential revenues they can make. For example, if they're allocated a challenging territory, they know that it's going to be harder work to penetrate and sell, and the chances of reaching their target may be smaller.

Defining and clearly understanding sales territories is key to the success of any sales compensation scheme.

The Definition Of A Sales Territory

Many people, both management and sales people, assume that sales territory refers to a specific geographic area. This is incorrect. Sales territories can be divided in several different ways, the most common being:

- By geographical area (such as by country or by state.)
- By industry (whether financial, education, software etc.)
- By clients (whether their account is a big or small one.)
- By account status (whether existing or new.)
- By products (where different salespeople focus on different products.)
- By project opportunity (where specific customer projects are the main focus.)

The Role Of Sales Territories In A Sales Compensation Plan

Sales compensation plans come in many forms. They may be commission based or bonus based. They might have a fixed portion and a variable portion. However, all sales compensation plans have one thing in common: Their purpose is to reward the sales force for their contribution to the company's profits, so they stay motivated. Each sales person has specific objectives they must reach (for example, bringing in $500,000 in sales from a specific territory by the end of the year.)

The sales territory and the compensation plan are linked together. Without one, the other would not be as effective. A compensation plan would make little sense if the sales people didn't know which territories they were covering, while knowing a sales territory doesn't mean much if sales people don't understand how the compensation plan applies to their territory.

I spoke recently with the head of sales for a tech company. He'd found that some of his sales people were frustrated with the incentives plans, and he was concerned about how that might affect their performance. An examination of the issue revealed that it wasn't the sales compensation plan that had them frustrated, but the territories they were being assigned. Now he knew where to look to solve the problem.

When a sales person is assigned an objective, the first thing they want to know is which territory they'll be working. Knowing the territory tells them whether or not the goal they've been set is achievable.

When To Allocate Territories

Before we talk about how to allocate territories, and how to deal with inequalities between territories, let's start right at the beginning: When to allocate territories.

The best time to assign territories is before the start of a new business year. This lets sales people familiarize themselves with their territories, which helps them perform at their best. Changing territories throughout the year is best avoided unless absolutely necessary.

Circumstances That Might Lead To A Mid-Year Territory Change

However, there are some times when a change in territory is needed during the current business year:

- When a salesperson leaves the company. This leaves deserted territories, and customers in those territories need a substitute sales person. Plus, some territories might lose momentum due to the salesperson leaving.

185

- When a new salesperson joins the sales force. Most new salespeople will already have experience in a prior territory. It's a smart idea to pay attention to that experience and allocate those salespeople to the territory best suited to them.
- When a certain territory is underperforming and management needs to respond quickly by changing the allocation of salespeople.
- When the company needs to implement a change in their strategy, especially one that requires shifting which sales territories get the most attention.
- When the target customer changes. Sometimes new trends, new laws, or other factors mean changing the target customer, or keeping existing target customers but working with them in a different way.
- When a new product is launched. A new product changes the revenue potential and dynamics of the company. As a result, salespeople may need to be allocated differently.

The Challenge Of Allocating Territories Fairly

There are many aspects to take into account when deciding how to allocate territories. The most common practice is to allocate them based on each salesperson's revenue potential and current performance. Their seniority is often a factor.

In some cases, it's better to involve the sales person and get their feedback – after all they know the dynamics of a territory inside and out.

However you do it, there's one challenge that always remains the same: That of how to allocate territories fairly.

All Sales People Need One Fundamental Thing

Sales people want to have equal opportunities for earning. They need to know that their earnings potential is similar to the rest of the sales team, and that they have the same chance as their colleagues to achieve that income.

Unfair treatment can lead to disgruntled employees who leave for pastures new. Many sales managers find themselves facing complaints that sales people don't feel their treatment is fair. Sometimes the problem comes down to the salesperson's own lack of commitment or performance. However, sometimes the problem is related to the territory, especially if it's hard to sell in, is an unmanageable size, or doesn't bring enough opportunities.

Sales is by nature a competitive field, and companies often encourage this. Internal competitions can keep sales people sharp and keep them striving to be the best.

For example, I know of a large IT company that hosts an exotic holiday for top achievers who have qualified for their elite President Sales Club each year. This highly sought-after prize is a challenge for even the most highly skilled sales people.

But imagine how frustrating it must be if the territories aren't equal? If those with challenging territories have much less chance to reach that prize? That's a quick route to frustration among sales staff, and a compelling argument for the importance of creating equal territories.

What Do Equal Territories Look Like?

Allocation of territories needs to be in line with company strategy, and also be fair to the sales people to avoid an imbalance of revenue opportunity.

Equal territories mean that each one is equal in terms of:

- The number of existing customers
- The number of potential new customers
- Revenues from existing customers
- Potential revenues from new customers
- Available selling time
- The amount of support and input the customers need
- Customer accessibility

Fair allocation of territories means that provided they put in a similar amount of effort, salespeople will have the chance to make similar earnings.

Say for example, your sales team is selling large scale technology to both the UK and Portugal. The UK offers more opportunities to sell, though, so management might need to adjust the quotas for each territory to make sure the earnings potential works out equal.

Factors To Take Into Account Before Allocating Territories

Before allocating territories, a company must carry out a thorough analysis of the following for each territory:

Demographics

- Is there a language barrier?
- How easy is access to the territory?
- What is the general mentality of customers there?
- What is the business culture?

Existing presence in that territory

- How many existing customers are there?
- What revenues do they bring in?
- Can you use references there?
- How strong are existing customer relations?

Business Potential

- How many institutions are there to sell to?
- How big are those institutions?
- What is the target market like?
- How many potential customers are there?
- What revenue is expected from them?

Personal factors

- How much selling time is available?

- How will sales people access the customers – will they need to travel extensively?

Companies should also assess which type of territory allocation best suits their needs. For example, if the key aim is to penetrate new geographic regions, then the focus should be on dividing territories by region. If the company provides solutions that are used by different industries, then allocation by industry makes sense. You can revisit the intro for a breakdown of the most common types of territory allocation.

Sales Factors To Consider

There are many sales factors that affect territory allocation. The role of management is to make decisions that guide the go-to market strategy, and offer the best potential to maximise revenues. Things to consider include:

- The business strategy and objectives.

- The future potential of each territory and product.

- The current market penetration and the opportunity to upsell and cross sell.

- The state of competition in the area.

- How saturated the market is.

How Do You Create A Level Playing Field For Your Sales Team?

Typically, a sales person is allocated an area of responsibility and a territory to work with. They have certain products to sell and an annual or a monthly target to meet. To be fair to each individual, each member of the sales team should be assigned a fair territory and a fair quota. The sales person needs to be clear about their territory and aims.

For example, a sales person may be given a target to bring in $20,000 revenue from existing customers, and develop ten new client relationships, regardless of the value of the product to be sold.

A clean and straightforward target, such as $1 million new revenue in a year, may be one of the first targets a sales manager gives to a sales person, after which the targets can be reviewed to suit the market and the territory.

About ten years ago I was involved with a technology company that had a sales force of around thirty staff, selling the same range of products in geographically defined territories throughout Europe. Some of the territories were defined by geography and others by industry. Naturally, some of the sales reps were selling to more promising regions in comparison to others that were trying to penetrate very difficult and unstable markets.

In situations like this, people soon get demoralized and turnover rises, especially among those who are allocated more challenging territories. After all, sales people still need to eat!

For those in more promising territories, loyalty increases. I met several reps who'd been there for seven years or more. So, the question then becomes, how do you create a level playing field for your sales team? This question can be further broken down into the following questions:

- When the sales team's job security is dependent on reaching targets, how do you ensure that all staff have fair and equal opportunities to succeed?

- When the top earners have the chance of a bonus, how do you make sure all sales staff have an equal chance at reaching that bonus?

- Are management fully aware of how different commission payments can be, even between people who've made the same sales effort, if territories are unequal?

- What is the overall attitude of the company regarding incentives schemes and territory allocation?

- Does the company want to pay sales people equally,

- whether or not sales people make similar effort, or

- when they bring similar revenues or

- when they bring similar successes?
- How can management reward sales people equally and fairly when they have different roles and dissimilar territories?

Territory and Quota Allocation

We have already seen the challenges presented to both management and the sales team with allocations of territories and sales targets. We've also talked about how setting sales targets that are out of reach can be counter-productive for the company and demoralizing for the sales team.

But how should one set the quota and handle the territory?

In my experience, I've found that an ideal set of targets is one which allows seventy percent of people to reach it. Assigned territories need to strike the balance between being challenging enough to keep the sales to keep sales teams motivated, but not so difficult as to frighten them away.

The most important thing to remember is the importance of assigning territories so that all sales staff have equal opportunities. To do otherwise can be a highly demotivation factor as a few sales people might be the privileged ones to get the best territories producing promising revenues, while others suffer and produce lesser results.

Solving The Problem Of Unfair Territories

In some ways a big territory may have more chance of producing more revenue. And with a traditional incentives and commission scheme that pays, for example, five percent to new gross revenues, a sales person who has a bigger territory has more chance to make more money.

Is this fair? How is that going to affect the morale of your sales people?

To solve this problem, the company must first decide whether all sales people should be given the same opportunity to earn. This is a fundamental question that needs to be answered in the early stages of implementing a sales motivation scheme. This is more of a business culture question than a technical one.

Here's a situation I came across recently:

A large company with a well-established brand name decided to launch a new product, and awareness of this new product was very limited in their target market. A sales person was hired to tackle the new market, and later the company realised this sales person had limited chances to make the same commissions that others were making, because the others were selling more established and recognised products.

How Should A Company Handle This Challenge?

If the company is willing to give equal revenue opportunity to sales people, although sales territories are different, there are technical ways to make earnings potential similar. Here are some common ways to solve the problem of unequal territories.

- Avoid having a system or part of the system that pays based on internal competition. It's better to make sure the responsibilities and territories between sales people are of similar dynamics.

- When territories are unequal, the problem can be resolved by optimizing the sales targets. Therefore a sales person with a more promising sales territory should have a more aggressive target than one who is covering, for example, a new market.

- Instead of paying commissions based on the actual value of the contracts, pay on target performance. For example, let's say John has a target of $1 million and Mary has a target of $2 million. Under a traditional scheme that pays up to sixty percent of target a commission of three percent and then up to and including a hundred percent a commission of eight percent, the payouts might look like this:

  John: 600,000 x 3% + 400,000 x 8% = 18,000 + 32,000 = $50,000

  Mary: 1,200,000 x 3% + 800,000 x 8% = 36,000 + 64,000 = $100,000

- According to this working, Mary will get more money in her pocket. But what if their company wants to pay them equally? In that case, they should be paid on the target realization and not the actual amount. The payment would be a percentage of the target incentive the job would pay.
- Let's say John and Mary have the same incentives target of $50,000 for reaching a hundred percent of target.
- The system could pay (for example) up to sixty percent of target realization, twenty percent of the target incentives, and then between sixty and a hundred percent of target realization, it would pay a hundred percent of target incentives.
- In the above example with John and Mary both reaching the target, they would get paid the same amount.
- Use a points system. That way more points can be assigned to a person that covers a more challenging territory. For example, the points might look like this:
- From 0-1,000 points pays $1 per point
- From 1,000-3,000 points pays $2 per point
- From 3,000 – 10,000 points pays $5 per point and so on
- The point system awards one point for dollar. If a sales person is in a difficult territory, it can be tweaked to give two points for every dollar sold.
- Associate the payment to the fixed salary of the sales person, provided the target associated with each sales person is correct. That way, the company can pay a percentage of salary for a hundred percent target performance. This technique uncouples the territory and instead pays according to target realization based on the fixed salary and total compensation the company wants to award the salesperson.
- Use a bonus scheme rather than a commission plan, which pays according to the dollar revenues a sales person brings. A bonus scheme works better

for dissimilar territories and roles, and allows for more subjective payment criteria.

In Conclusion

Dealing with dissimilar sales territories can be a headache, but with effort and focus it can be fixed. Fair warning: If you don't invest the extra effort to find a workable solution, you might find yourself creating a situation of demotivation and disappointment that leads to a high turnover. If, however, you put in the time and apply some outside of the box thinking, you can create a solution that works.

Always keep these three points in mind:

- Territories are not similar in terms of potential and revenue forecast.
- Sales people want to maximize their potential.
- Sales people want equal opportunities to earn.

Territory assignment is a vital part of developing a sales compensation plan. It required constant monitoring by sales management in order to deliver optimum results. It's often the case that complaints about the incentive plan actually lead back to bad territory allocation.

By applying the techniques in this article, you can create a level playing field that's both fair and motivational, benefitting both the sales team and the company.

Moving To A New Scheme – Changing Your Status Quo And How To Transit To A New Era With Less Pain

Most sales organisations change their sales incentives scheme at some point, or at least wonder if they should. This is normal – incentives schemes are dynamic, and ought to grow and change with the company. A sales scheme directly mirrors the management's objectives, and if those objectives shift, so the sales scheme might need to as well.

Changing to a new motivation scheme is a major undertaking. Many problems might arise if the changeover isn't handled the right way. However, not changing scheme when you need to can also cause problems.

In this paper we'll take a look at how to tell it's time to change your motivation scheme, and what you can do to make the changeover as painless and effective as possible.

The Very Real Problems Of Changing Sales Scheme

Let's start by looking at the real problems that can arise when changing sales schemes. Knowing these means you can be alert to them, and design the implementation of your new scheme to avoid these issues.

There are all real problems faced by companies I have worked with.

Case 1: This company made some amendments and released the new scheme to the sales force. Shortly after, many of their staff members left.

Case 2: Another company made changes to their scheme and were confused to find that their sales team were no longer selling their newly-launched product, but were promoting a different one.

Case 3: One company was horrified to realise that they were spending considerably more money in incentives on their new scheme than expected.

Case 4: Finally, this company didn't change their sales scheme. They were struggling with poor results and seeing their objectives go unreached, not realizing that the problem was their sales scheme.

Changing to a new sales scheme feels like leaping into the dark. No one knows if it will work or how effective it will be. When problems arise, managers are often left baffled as to what went wrong.

Let's look at how to make a clear decision on whether to move to a new scheme, and how to boost the chances of the new scheme succeeding. That way we cut down guesswork and it's easier to meet goals with the new scheme.

Is Changing System Really Worth It?

All this talk of the problems that arise with changing the motivation scheme might leave you wonder if it's really worth it. Maybe it's better to just stick with the system you currently have?

Absolutely not. Changing motivation scheme as and when required puts you ahead of the competition, because you're changing your system to best fit your objectives and make sure you meet them.

The key is to know when the time is right to make a change, and to plan the switchover carefully. And it starts with assessing your current system.

Start With Assessing Your Current System

To know whether you need to change sales scheme, you first have to assess the system you currently have. In fact, I'd say this goes beyond assessment into monitoring.

I recommend every company that relies heavily on a sales team sets up a specific task force for keeping an eye on the sales scheme. Their task is to monitor the existing motivation scheme, including the activities of the sales team and the results they get. This specialist team should also note down any possible problems. One of the best ways to monitor problems is to keep a record of turnover of sales people, and to have an exit interview with each departing team member so they can find out the reasons behind their decision.

So you set up your team, and make clear that their role is to assess the system and make suggestions for improvement.

Now you need to give them the necessary tools to monitor and assess the system. Make sure they have access to all the data and tools necessary for both qualitative and quantitative monitoring.

Regular monitoring is the quickest way to flag up issues. For example, if your task force is monitoring how often sales people reach their targets, and they find that ninety percent of your sales staff have an average performance of 130 percent, that shows something is amiss. Targets are too easy to reach – so the sales scheme needs to be changed.

Six Signs That You Need A New Motivation Scheme

Many people are change-averse. Sales managers might find themselves wondering if they really need to change their sales system, especially if they've changed it recently and the results of the change were disappointing.

In my time working with sales teams and helping them make decisions about their sales schemes, I've noticed six key indicators surface time and time again. These signs all point to the fact that you need to consider changing your motivation scheme.

1. Sales people are quitting their jobs at an unacceptable rate. Yes sales people might quit their jobs for different reasons, but not being properly motivated by the incentives scheme is a top reason.

2. The results your company is getting are not aligned with management objectives. For example, if your management team decided to increase sales of a certain product by ten percent, but in fact sales for that project are dropping.

3. One group of sales people are earning considerably more in commissions than some of their team mates. This breeds resentment and a feeling of unfairness among the sales team, which is bad for overall morale.

4. Incentive payments are taking far too long to reach sales staff. If your sales team are expecting to see their incentives within a month, but having to wait four or five months, they might start looking for a new job.

5. The company is having to pay considerably more in incentives and commissions to reach the same goals as before.

6. It seems like the only way to make the sales force more effective is to give more and more money through incentives.

This isn't an exhaustive list – some companies have problems specific only to them that still indicate a need for change – but these are certainly some of the most common indicators that it's time to change the scheme.

Identifying Which Part Of The Scheme To Change

Often, identifying which technical parts of the scheme you need to change, is the hardest part of changing sales scheme. An incentives scheme has many moving parts, and each part plays a role in the overall workings of the scheme. So how do you figure out which part to change?

Let's take a look at some of the different sales scheme mechanics that you might have in your own scheme, and which might need changing.

For example, your current scheme might link together two performance measures, either as a multiplier or as a hurdle. If they're linked as a multiplier, then a sales person who achieves target A will get a multiplier in the performance of target B. But if they're linked as a hurdle, then the sales person much accomplish target A in order to be paid for target B.

Some schemes work on the basis of a cap, where there is a limit to the incentives paid. If a sales person sells above the cap, they don't make any more money.

These are just two of the ways a sales scheme might work. If you notice there is a problem with your sales scheme, those are two places you might look for a solution.

Let's look at another example, and how it applies to changing the scheme.

Let's say that you realise ninety percent of your sales team are meeting 150 percent of their targets. Clearly that number is too high, but how do you decide which part of the scheme to change?

It's easy to say, well, you're paying too much in commissions, so just don't pay incentives over a hundred percent. But then, sales people will not be motivated. Once they hit a hundred percent of their sales, they'll simply stop trying so hard, because there's nothing in it for them.

But there isn't just one solution to the problem of over inflated commissions. Another way to solve it is to set better targets. You can monitor your targets and amend them if it seems like they're too easy to reach. In this scenario, you might still choose to pay commissions for sales over a hundred percent, because fewer people will be reaching those targets, and you'll be rewarding the very best sales staff and keeping them loyal to your company.

Another solution is to add an entry threshold. For example, put in a threshold of sixty percent so sales people don't start getting commission until they reach sixty percent of their performance. That way, they are still motivated to sell, even if they don't try to sell above a hundred percent.

The design of a sales compensation scheme requires technical knowledge. It's not just a managerial decision. When assessing your current scheme and deciding what, if anything, to change, always seek the opinion of people who know about sales scheme design and can advise you on how to achieve better specific results.

Keep the technicalities of your sales scheme in mind at all times and assess each area of it thoroughly. That way, you can be confident that you're changing the right part of it.

You Don't Always Have To Reinvent The Wheel

Before we look at planning a change to the sales scheme, I want to point out that not every problem indicates that the entire sales scheme needs to change.

Sometimes, only a small change is necessary. That's why I recommend starting with thorough assessment and monitoring of the existing scheme, so you can see where the problem lies and what needs to be done.

When deciding what to change, always keep in mind that any change, big or small, will affect certain groups of sales people. It's impossible to change motivation scheme in a way that leaves every single sales person better off. Before any change, be sure you understand who it will affect and how. Be realistic about how such a change is likely to affect the sales force, and your results.

I recommend making small changes to the sales scheme as often as necessary to keep the scheme aligned with your company's objectives.

Of course, as this article shows, sometimes a big change is truly necessary. By a big change I mean something like:

- Moving from a bonus system to a commission system.

- Moving from individual incentives to team incentives.

- Bringing in payments for other sales people who contribute to selling a specific product, thus splitting commission between more people.

I recommend that such big changes only take place once every two or three years. Big changes take time to plan, implement, and settle in. Changing more frequently will only lead to confusion and dissatisfaction, for sales staff and management alike.

Let's take a look at how to identify changes that need to be made, and then how to communicate them to your sales staff.

The Four Rules To Follow Before Changing Motivation Scheme

Keeping these four simple rules in mind when you want to change your sales scheme, will help the change go much more smoothly.

1. Assess. Always think through the change carefully. Be sure that you know exactly what the problem is, and that you're confident a change in the motivation scheme is the answer.

2. Evaluate. You have a change in mind that you want to make. Now take time to evaluate the results you're anticipating from this change. Will this change truly tackle the issue? Will it get you the results you need?

3. Consider. Think about the consequences of making this change. Think about which members of your sales team will suffer negative consequences from the change you want to make. Often making a change fixes one problem, but creates another. For example, if you lower commission rates to fix the problem of overspending on incentive payments, you might find sales people don't like their new incentive payments, and you end up with higher staff turnover.

4. Communicate. Before you change the scheme, it's vital to communicate your intentions. Start by talking about it with your line managers. Once you're sure the change is going ahead, communicate it to your sales team – don't wait till after to tell them!

Be Aware Of The Possible Negative Consequences

I could have put this under point three above, but it's important enough to warrant further expansion.

No matter how good your intentions for changing your sales scheme, there is always the risk of negative consequences.

That's the bad news. The good news is that often these negative consequences happen because managers didn't properly think through the consequences of the change. That's why proper planning and evaluation is so important.

Here are some common negative consequences to be aware of at the planning stage:

- Higher sales staff turnover
- Staff underperforming on certain objectives
- Sales staff getting caught up in certain activities to the detriment of other parts of their job
- Dissatisfied clients and higher client turnover
- Losing part of your market share
- Compensation scheme costs more to run
- Sales staff not understanding the system
- Administration taking more effort and costing more
- Late payment of incentives
- A sense of unfairness between parts of the sales team

From my experience in working with many different companies, I know that any change to the sales scheme brings with it the risk of negative effects. Sometimes this is due to a glitch in the system, and sometimes it's to do with how sales staff perceive the new system.

This isn't to put you off changing sales scheme. Rather, by being aware of all the potential consequences you can take steps to mitigate them before launching the new scheme, thus increasing your chances of success.

Create An Operational Time Line

Good planning is key to changing your sales scheme effectively. I suggest setting out an operational time line for your changes. Make sure this time line is properly recorded, and that everyone involved is familiar with the time line and is sticking to it.

Your operational document should describe exactly who is responsible for what. Often, there are many people involved in changing the sales scheme, from the CEO to HR, finance, and sales managers. It's important that everyone is on board before you begin. If any part of the process needs approval from someone else, get those approvals before you start first.

Changing the sales scheme can take as long as three or even six months. Just imagine the amount of analysis, evaluation, recommendation, and consideration of all the moving parts, that entails! Having your time line, responsibilities, and approvals in place before you begin will make the process much smoother.

Rushing or leaving parts of the process to the last minute will not help your company make the transition. Map out a realistic time line and make sure everyone involved knows all their responsibilities and deadlines. Planning is everything.

Seven Key Steps For Communicating The Change To Your Sales Team

The most important part of the time line is communicating the new system to the sales force. That part needs to be planned and carried out with great attention to detail, if the new scheme is to work.

Sales teams don't take kindly to a change in the sales scheme. It's easy to see why – now they have to relearn the system, figure out how it affects their territory and product, and make sure they're selling in such a way as to maximize the money they can now make.

When sales people are used to a system, they can predict with some accuracy how much money they're likely to make. Changing the scheme can leave sales staff feeling unsettled, as that security has now gone. They might be wondering, is this really better for me? What if I can't make as much money?

Whether you're making a small change or overhauling your entire system, communication to your sales staff is vital.

Communication takes just as much planning as any other part of the process. After all, your sales staff are the ones who need to use the new scheme every day. If you don't make the changeover easy for them, your company will suffer.

Here are seven tips that I've found effective for communicating the change:

1. Plan your communication properly. Don't do anything unplanned. Think about what you will say, and how you will say it.

2. Be truthful. If the reason for the new plan is because you want to pay less incentives, say so. People might not like it, but dishonesty will harm your working relationship far more.

3. Explain the change. There's always a reason for changing an incentives scheme. Be direct with your sales staff about the reason for the change.

4. Ask for their feedback. Your sales staff's opinions matter, so ask for feedback, and take it on board.

5. Sell the big idea. After all, the overall plan for the change is to create positive results for the company. Even if there are no obvious short-term positives, show your sales people the long-term benefits of the change.

6. Offer continuous support. So many companies tell their sales people about the change but don't follow up. Essentially, they tell them "this is what we're doing, learn to live with it." My experience has shown me that companies who have a transition period (as much as six months if needed) get better results.

7. Never communicate important changes via email. Call a meeting and tell your sales staff the changes face to face.

Test The System In Real Time

Now you've assessed, planned, and communicated your new scheme, there's one last thing to do: **Test it in real time.**

Any change to the system could affect another part of the system, and sometimes in unexpected ways. That's why you need to monitor the change in real time.

One technology company I know was struggling with underselling of a new product. So, managers decide to launch a separate commission scheme for the new product, giving generous incentives for selling it. It seemed like a good idea at the time, but before long sales of their other product lines were dropping fast, while sales of the new products soared. Sale staff were jumping at the chance to make the new, bigger commissions, and neglecting the other, lower-paying products.

Their choice just wasn't the right fix for the issue. If they had tested the scheme straight away, they would have spotted the problem before it got out of hand.

There are two main things you must do to assess the system:

1. Assess the system and think thoroughly about how the proposed changes will affect the performance of the system.

2. Run theoretical and assumed scenarios of future performances so you can test how the system reacts.

One way to bridge the gap between testing and real use of the system is to use and calculate incentives using both systems. If it turns out that monthly payments are too low or high using the new system, pay according to the old system while the bugs are worked out.

Another way of doing this is to apply the new system for three months, but still pay according to the old system. During this period, communicate the results to your sales staff using the new system so they can see for themselves how it works and how their effort relates to the amount they get paid.

Any change is difficult. People don't like change, especially because they can't predict any negative effects it might have on their payments.

However, change in motivation scheme is essential. A dynamic firm that wants to keep growing and meeting new objectives needs their sales motivation scheme to grow and change with them.

Thorough assessment and planning will help you foresee potential problems and decide what to do about them.

Whatever you do, make sure your sales compensation design team is on board, They know the system and its consequences better than anyone, and have the skills to see which changes would most benefit your company.

And always, always listen to your sales people and keep them in the loop. They know more about using the scheme than anyone, and if they're on board with the new scheme, it has much better chances of succeeding.

Administration Of A Sales Incentives Program; The Internal Governance, The Committees And Their Responsibilities. How To Make Sure You Achieve Smooth Operation Of The System

I know the administration of sales schemes isn't an exciting topic, and the implementation can seem long drawn out and boring. However, the success of an incentives program hinges on the administration process. If you don't think it through, the administration could scupper the whole program.

I once met with the head of sales of a fintech company. They had a team of fifteen people with an incentives scheme in place. I asked her whose job it was to alert her if there was a problem, and what processes were in place for deciding and signing off on changes to the system. She looked at me like I was talking a foreign language - it turned out her company had no one in charge of flagging problems, analysing results, or proposing changes. I knew that was where some of her problems with her sales incentives scheme were coming from.

She's by no means the only exec I've met who had no administration scheme in place. This can cause serious problems in the running of a sales incentives scheme.

Five Problems That Stem From Lack Of Administration

Lack of administration in a sales scheme is a common problem, and it has several negative effects. Here are five common problems that stem from lack of sales administration:

- **Staff being frustrated at the lack of support.** If no one is in charge, or the people in charge are not well suited to it, sales staff get frustrated. I once worked with a company who had handed admin to their HR department. That left their sales staff with no one who truly understood the scheme to turn to with technical questions, exemption requests, or any other problems. As a result, sales staff were leaving the company.

- **Delayed payments.** I've worked with several companies whose sales staff were frustrated by late payments, sometimes as much as two or three months late. It turned out the admin was too complicated and it was hard to calculate incentives, so the team were getting behind on paying them.

- **Difficulty making good future decisions.** To make good decisions about the future of a sales scheme, you need solid reporting. If there's no one assessing and reporting on the current scheme, then managers don't have the information they need to adjust the scheme for the future.

- **Lack of procedures**. I worked with a company who had just two people controlling the entire sales scheme, from design to payment. The procedures weren't transparent, and there was no formal way of making decisions. When we audited their sales incentives, we found the lack of procedures meant the administration of the scheme was inconsistent.

- **Improper documentation.** I walked into one company and found that there was no documentation related to the incentives scheme. The scheme had been drafted in some emails, and the design written down on a piece of paper! No documentation means no ownership of the scheme, and more mistakes both in the administration of the scheme, and in communicating it.

The Five Steps To Effective Sales Scheme Administration

Many managers fall into the trap of thinking the incentives program starts with the design and ends with payment distribution. In fact, there is much more to it than that. It starts with a team of designers working for a common goal, takes a journey through excellent governance and clear communication with the sales staff, and ends with assessments and auditing.

There are five steps that every company must follow if they want to effectively administrate their sales scheme:

- Setting up committees
- Calculating incentives

- Writing policies and documents
- Reporting
- Auditing

When all these steps are followed, a sales steam has a much higher chance of success, thanks to proper administration. Let's take a look at each one.

Setting Up Committees

Running a sales scheme takes time and effort. It's not a job for one or two people. It requires the involvement of people from several different departments, each of whom has their role to play.

Setting up the right committees makes it easier to create a workable framework, and then run the scheme properly once it's built.

Which Committees To Set Up

I suggest every company sets up the following four teams:

- Design team. They're responsible for assessing the current scheme and recommending how to alter it, and designing the new scheme. This is usually formed from a combination of salespeople, HR staff, finance staff, and a member of the CEO office.
- The owner of the scheme. This isn't a team, but one person who is responsible for the current program. They're not the decision maker, but they are responsible for smooth operation of the system.
- Commission overseers. This is a separate team from the design committee, whose job it is to give feedback on the sales scheme design, and weigh in on proposals and changes. This gives the design team an outside view, which is invaluable.

- Data analysis team. These are the people tasked with analysing data, running analysis on the current system, and identifying problems and strengths. This team should be comprised of competent data analysts who are confident with assessing data.

Calculating Incentives

Calculating incentives isn't only about deciding what to pay sales people. it's also about analysing key performance indicators to show the effectiveness of the system.

Systems data can be used to directly calculate the incentives to be paid. It can also be analysed in order to gather data to help management make decisions on the future of the system. From here, management can decide what data they need, what systems to use for calculations, and which team members are needed to carry those out.

Important Areas To Consider

Here are some areas to consider when calculating incentives.

Know who's in charge of calculating incentives. This can either be done manually using database systems such as Excel, or using a sales system. The latter is a better choice for sales teams bigger than twenty five people. Make sure there's a team allocated to this task.

Look out for these three common pitfalls when calculating incentives:

- Deviation from the ideal target figures. In most cases, two thirds of people should be reaching their quotas, with ten percent reaching a level of excellence above the others. Keep a close eye on any deviations from this.
- Be mindful of double payments. Sometimes a mistake is made leading to a double payment. In addition, complex sales cycles can lead to two people being paid for the same deal, when only one should have been paid.

- Unethical sales. Unfortunately, this does happen sometimes. Sales people might try to manipulate the system to get a bigger payment, such as by overcharging customers or selling them products they don't really need. The calculation team should keep an eye on sales to flag up any suspicious activity.

Be mindful of deadlines. Teams must be careful of deadlines when calculating incentives, to ensure payroll has the information they need to make timely payments to sales staff.

Be clear on what data to gather. Some performance measures are hard to get data for. For example, if the incentives scheme pays $100 for an increase in customer satisfaction, how is that customer satisfaction measured? When deciding on a target or incentive, always make sure it is clear what data is needed and how it is to be collected.

Ensure everyone knows their roles, and who to turn to. You'll need an organisational chart of the team that lists everyone's individual responsibilities.

Writing Policies and Documenting Processes

I once worked with a company that had carefully documented their payments policy, and yet it seemed that incentives calculation and payment were not lining up with that policy.

The incentives plan had a threshold of sixty percent. That meant that in order to get paid, a salesperson had to reach at least sixty percent of their target. Sales people who were getting near but not quite reaching sixty percent would complain about only just missing out on a payment, and in some cases the sales manager would approve a payment for those reaching fifty seven to fifty nine percent of their target.

The problem was there was no consistency. The company had an incentives policy but hadn't included a specific policy for exemptions. No one knew exactly how to treat those who were nearly at their target, how to treat exemption requests, or even who was responsible for approving the requests. Once they got a policy in place, incentives calculation went much more smoothly.

Policies That Need To Be Documented

As the above example shows, failing to properly document part of the process can cause problems in the sale scheme. Here are the policies that every sales team needs to decide upon and properly document:

- **The approval process.** There should be a workflow diagram in place that shows who is responsible for approving changes to the plan, and exemption requests.

- **Exception policy.** Like in our example above, every organisation needs a document that sets out when exceptions may be given and who is responsible for approving those.

- **Auditing policy.** Most sales schemes need to be audited every three to six months, and this process should be fully documented.

- **Design and analysis.** A company should thoroughly document every policy concerning the design and analysis of the system.

- **Responsibilities.** Companies should draw up a stakeholder document that sets out who is part of each team, and their responsibilities.

Once the documents are drafted, it's important that they're maintained. If the system changes in any way, so the relevant documents must also be changed to stay up to date.

Two Important Documents Every Company Must Have

Every company needs a policy document and a workflow chart.

The policy document contains all the important information about the current sales system, and should include:

- Details about both the current scheme and the previous versions of it;

- A log of any changes and amendments to the sales incentives scheme;

- Sales crediting;
- The approval process;
- Program timing;
- Auditing policy;
- How territories are allocated and what happens if there is a change in territories;
- The reporting that the data analysis team are expected to carry out and what data they should use for it;
- How quota management is decided, including the quota approval process and the policy to follow if a sales person leaves or accounts get reshuffled, or anything else happens to change quotas;
- Exception policy;
- Policy to follow during a transition period including how changes to the system are to be communicated and implemented; and
- The rights and obligations of both sales people and management.

The workflow chart covers all the processes in the sales scheme, which brings full transparency to the scheme and its administration. Each company needs a workflow for:

- Accountability and ownership. Who is responsible for each aspect of the scheme, and how and when should they act.
- The timing of the scheme, such as when incentives will be calculated and paid.

Proper writing and updating of policies and documents means there's much less room for mistakes and anomalies, and the sales scheme will run much more smoothly.

Reporting

Good reporting is a key part of analysing the system and giving feedback to management. Reporting arms management with the information they need to:

- Spot issues;
- Assess the efficiency of the sales scheme;
- Identify whether the system is improving or deteriorating the company overall;
- See whether the system is properly aligned with company objectives and culture;
- Assess how costly the system is and whether it's proving to be worth the cost of implementing it; and
- Decide on the best action to take to make sure the scheme works as well as possible.

When setting up systems for reporting, it's important to decide what kind of reporting needs to be done, and who needs access to the information. That includes deciding on which KPIs will most help with assessing the system.

Always bear in mind that reporting isn't just about gathering figures but rather about gathering data that can be used to analyse problems and challenges, and make changes.

Here are some of the most common reports that most sales-focused companies need to generate:

- Administrator reports (log of exceptions, audit reporting, credit, quota and territory).
- Senior management reports (cost of incentives, effectiveness and performance).
- Field sales management report with the necessary data set and analysis given back to sales people and their immediate management.

- Product management (product performance, and how sales people are performing for each product line).
- HR (how payments compare to the market overall, and how payments are related to retention, turnover, and sales team satisfaction).
- Finance (cost of incentives and cost vs. budget so that the company can stay within their forecast budgets).
- Executives reports (generic performance and synopsis of above plus some indicative problems).

The reports may differ depending on whose desk they're destined for. For example, the CEO will be interested in the effectiveness of incentives from a different angle than the finance team or the human resources. Different reports can be generated for:

- Senior management (incl. CEO)
- Sales managers
- Product management
- Finance
- HR
- Executives

Auditing

Commission and bonus payments are a large financial outgoing for any company, so it's vital that the sales scheme is properly audited to be sure money is being spent wisely. Most companies require a sales scheme audit every three to six months.

Every audit should answer the following questions:

- Are payments being distributed according to the plan? Is the plan being properly followed?

- Are there any exemptions to the sale scheme (such as for those almost reaching their targets, or those far out-performing them) and how are those being handled?
- Are there proper committees, ownership, and approval procedures in place for the system?
- Is the calculation, administration, and operation function of the system being adequately manned?
- Are there any major problems that need attention such as a significant increase in high payments or increased sales staff turnover?
- Is everything being properly documented, from policies to administration?
- Is there a proper system in place for documenting previous versions of the scheme and changes to it?

In particular, any audit needs to monitor:

- Whether payments are being made according to policy, how payments are being calculated, and whether there are any mistakes being made.
- How many exemption requests are being made and how those are handled.
- How sales crediting is carried out, especially for complex sales involving more than one person or department.
- The design of the scheme and how adjustments are made.
- All procedures and whether they're being properly followed and documented.

Auditing is a clear and unbiased method for making sure that payment rules are correctly set according to both company policy and market standards, and that those rules are being followed. To this end, auditors should pay particular attention to:

- Unethical sales

- Double payments
- Fraud

The auditing team should be independent from the sales team, but should also have experience and knowledge of incentives schemes. The best thing is to set up a formal audit committee and set out a specific time line of audits to be performed. The committee should look at every part of the system.

It's not the role of the audit committee to say whether or not the system is efficient. Once they present their results to management, it's the role of management to identify the best person to resolve any issues raised. The resolution of all audit cases should be part of the audit process document.

Setting up the administration side of a sales scheme, from committees to documents and processes, takes time. However, it's time well spent, because without correct administration a company stands to lose much more in the way of payments, sales staff, and time wasted on frustrations and problems further down the line.

Communicating The Plan; Why Should You Care And Why This Is Extremely Important To Consider

Every Company Needs The Right Motivation Scheme

Every single company relies on revenues – that's just common sense. The role of the sales force is to sell products and bring in those revenues. This is the heart of any organisation that sells something, and without a good sales team and strong results, a company could be in trouble.

A sales motivation scheme gives sales people an incentive to do well and bring in plenty of revenue. There are lots of ways to design a sales motivation scheme, including bonus, commission based, pools and more.

A sales motivation scheme needs to be designed to best serve the company. It's one of the biggest and most powerful tools to hand for supporting the sales process and bringing the right results. Sales schemes can't be designed in an afternoon or one quick meeting. There are so many different elements to consider, including thresholds, linkages and caps, to name but a few.

For companies that sell multiple products in different ways, sales schemes get even more complex.

Sales people need to be well versed in the way the motivation plan works. It can take a while to get familiar with the system, and sales people often find themselves with multiple pages to read and digest.

Sometimes, a sales scheme isn't working and the company needs to design a new one. That in itself is a time-consuming process, but companies sometimes forget one of the most important elements – how to communicate the new scheme to the sales force.

Communicating The Sales Scheme Matters – A Lot

The way a company communicates its new sales motivation scheme is just as important as the design of the scheme itself. Think of it this way: It's very similar to selling a product to customers. Even if the product is the best, most innovative, product that's ideal for the customers' needs, the company still needs to figure out how to position the product and sell it to the market.

It's the same with communicating a new sales scheme, except now the product is the scheme and the customers are the sales force. How it's positioned and sold to them impacts how they respond to it, how well they understand it, and ultimately how successful it is. Companies need to consider who tells the sales force about the scheme, and what they say about it. They need to think about how the information will be received. After all, they need the majority of the sales force to "buy" the new concept, and act on it.

Management needs to give some thought to how to do this, and pay close attention to the reaction they get. Are employees paying attention? Are they grasping the new system? Do they have a lot of questions and, most importantly, do they know who to address their questions to?

A lack of poor communication can negatively affect a company, and bring less than stellar results. That's why, when designing a new sales scheme, it's important to design the delivery of it to the sales force, too. In this article we'll look at the important points companies should consider, and some tips to make sure the process goes smoothly.

Keep These Three Aims In Mind

As you design your communication plan, keep these three outcomes in mind.

1. Every person in the sales force is well informed about the new plan and ready to engage with the new incentive scheme.

2. Every person in the sales force understands how the new scheme relates directly to their selling goals and activities. For example, if management wants sales people to concentrate on cross-selling to existing accounts, the onus is on managers to make sure their staff understand how the new scheme helps them to do that.

3. Every person in the sales force has a thorough understanding of the new system, as evidenced by their sales behaviour and activity.

The ultimate aim of communicating the new system is to have at least eighty percent of sales people following the new scheme properly. It's natural for some people in the sales force to have issues with implementation, but a figure of at least eighty percent understanding is a helpful benchmark. If it's below that, managers should look to problems both in the scheme and in the way it was communicated (we'll look at some causes of poor communication shortly.)

Dangers Of Not Communicating The System Properly

As we've established, the sales compensation scheme is a core part of any organisation that sells products, and issues with the scheme lead to less than optimal performance. Frankly, sales scheme problems equal less money in the bank – an outcome no one is happy with.

I see the sales scheme as a communication tool between management and their sales force. It wouldn't make sense for managers to meet and speak with each sales person about sales strategy. Instead, the incentive plan acts as a bridge, showing sales people what goals management has set, and how they expect their people to reach those goals.

If people aren't properly informed about the sales scheme, it's easy for them to start losing direction. A thorough understanding of the plan makes it easier for sales people to follow the vision of their company. The plan is the main guideline they have for fulfilling their part in that mission, so a good understanding of it is key.

Of course, people who don't understand the system might simply ignore it. This is bad news for everyone! If twenty percent of the sales people are simply ignoring the system, that means twenty percent of the sales force are immediately in danger of not meeting their targets. There's also a risk that they'll carry out steps in the process incorrectly, or skip them altogether.

As time goes on, people who don't understand the scheme are going to produce less, meet less targets, and eventually jeopardize not only their own targets, but the goals of the whole company. If this keeps up, those sales people are going to lose their motivation, start missing opportunities to make money, and eventually go looking for a new job. High sales staff turnover isn't good for any company.

One of the biggest dangers of not communicating properly is the loss of confidence and trust between management and their sales staff. The incentive scheme is the most important sales tool management has to lead the sales force in the right direction and encourage them to meet targets. If those sales people don't understand the scheme and can't meet their targets with it, they'll blame management (and in many cases they would be right to – the onus is on management to make sure their team understands.) Now the trust between them is damaged and the professional relationship is broken. It's hard to gain back that trust when it's gone, which is why it's much better to communicate clearly in the first place.

The Three Top Causes Of Poor Communication

Poor communication of a new sales scheme is usually caused by one of three things:

1. The most common cause is that management don't plan how to tell people about the new scheme. They just send out an email and expect that to be enough, without providing any further clarification or letting sales people what to do if they have questions.

2. They tell sales people there's a new scheme, but don't tell them why. Sales people are far more likely to make the effort to use the new scheme if they understand why the change was made, and why it's important to both their targets and the overall company targets.

3. Management doesn't follow up with their sales team after the initial communication. I've seen so many managers send an email and expect their staff to start using the system, without following up to make sure they understand what to do.

Now we know how important it is to communicate the new sales plan correctly, let's go through some things managers need to consider before communicating to the sales force.

Keep These Main Rules In Mind

As you plan how to communicate about your new sales scheme, it helps to keep these main rules in mind:

- Make sure the communication is simple and easy to understand. Sales people shouldn't need extensive technical notes or a glossary to understand it.

- Keep your communication as short, constructive, and to the point as possible.
- Give clear examples of how payments work under the new system.
- Explain the differences from the new system – both what they are and why management made the changes.
- Explain the math behind the incentive formulas, and the reason for using those specific terms.
- Give the sales force reasons to care about the new scheme – let them know why it matters to them, how it impacts them, and how it can help them better reach their targets.

Decide Who Will Communicate The New System

Now you know the main rules to follow, it's time to decide who in charge of communicating the new sales scheme. I find the very best person for the job is nearly always the head of sales. After all, the compensation scheme is a sales management tool, so what better person to deliver it than the head of sales?

The job of the head of sales is to direct the sales force and make sure they meet their targets, for the good of the whole company. The sales scheme is one of the main ways for sales managers to direct their sales team, so it makes sense that they should be the one to announce any changes to the scheme.

Communicating with their team about the new motivation plan also gives the sales manager to communicate his strategy and aims for the new plan, and share his vision of how the new plan will work both now and in the future. This clear and direct communication is beneficial to everyone involved, and helps build trust between the sales manager and the sales force.

List What Information To Include

One of the pitfalls of communicating about a new motivation plan is giving the wrong information. Sometimes the problem is not enough information, and the sales force is missing some vital pieces that would make their job much easier.

Sometimes the problem is too much information, leaving the sales force bogged down in facts and feeling like they'll never understand the new plan.

A useful rule of thumb is this: Just because it was discussed in a board meeting, doesn't mean it needs to be passed on to the sales force.

Managers should take some time to sift through all the information they have about the new scheme and refine it, picking out only that which the sales people really need to know.

Every single piece of information shared should have a link to the motivation scheme, how to use it, and its purpose. For example, if the new scheme strongly favours income from new clients, sales people need to know this. It's also helpful for them to understand why the new system leans this way, and how it relates to company targets.

Here are some things that should be included with every communication about the new sales scheme:

Strategy. Let sales people know what the company's current strategy is. Set out what the company is looking to achieve in both qualitative and quantitative terms. This includes sales figures but also other aims such as bringing a new product to market, or developing a new product for existing customers.

Changes. Make sure sales people understand all of the changes from the previous motivation scheme. Draw attention to all the new elements, and explain to the sales staff the importance of tweaking their selling process to fit the new features. For example, if there is a new entry barrier of performance to earn commission, make sure this is clear.

Justification. No one likes being told to just do something, with no explanation as to why. Talk to your sales staff about why the scheme is changing. Make sure you clearly spell out how the new scheme relates to the company's overall aims. Don't assume that sales staff will just guess at the reason for changes – write it down clearly. Understanding the why makes it more likely that they'll put the scheme into practice.

Effect. Make sure everyone understands the way the new scheme affects the money and commissions they earn. Give some example scenarios and show the sales results that would happen in each of this scenario. I suggest giving three examples, quite different from one another, with a clear note of what the final commission would be in each case. Communicate how the changes will affect low, average, and high performers. Don't ever be tempted to skip over parts that you think won't go down well – the breach of trust from being lied to by management is more damaging than hearing bad news about the new scheme.

Think About How To Sell The New System

The ultimate aim is for the sales team to feel happy about the new system, though of course that might not happen right away. One way to increase the chances of them embracing the new system, is to think about how to sell it to them.

Always remember that the role of the motivation scheme is to do exactly what its name says – keep people motivated. If they aren't motivated, they will ignore the system or implement it only half-heartedly.

That's why managers need to truly sell the system to their staff. The sales force needs to truly understand what's in it for them. Why should they use the system? What benefits will be using it bring them in both the short and the long term?

The aim of any sales motivation scheme is to increase a company's revenues. From the point of view of the sales staff, this means more money in their pockets. It means more money for the things they want, be that savings, a vacation, a new home, or to pursue a project they love. So, show them how the scheme increases their chances of getting good commission. Make it worth their while to throw themselves behind the new system.

What To Do After Communicating The New Scheme

You now know that sending out the communication and not following up is one of the most common mistakes managers make when implementing a new sales motivation scheme. Here's what to do instead.

First, make sure that everyone has been informed about the new system. Every single sales person is an important member of the team, and their performance contributes to the overall results the team gets. So, make sure everyone knows about it. Line managers should check that all sales people have received the new system.

Next, make sure that the new system and its workings and rules are clear to everybody. Each team member should be given time to sit down with their

223

supervisor and talk about the new system. Yes, these sessions are time consuming, but they're an important part of making sure the whole team understands. They also make sure each person in the sales force feels heard.

Now everyone knows about the system and has had the chance to talk with their supervisor, establish a team that's responsible for answering questions and providing support as the new system is bedded in. Rather than wait for questions to come, I suggest setting up time for a group Q&A where people can ask their questions. This could also be done by asking people to email in their questions. After, create an FAQ that answers all the questions, and send a copy to every person in the sales force. If line managers need to send out technical documents explaining the system further, an FAQ is a good way to make the document easier to digest.

Ask the sales team for feedback. Find out whether they like it or not, and why. People naturally don't like change, and are risk averse. It's normal for people to be nervous or unhappy about changes to the sales system. Managers can ease this anxiety by explaining the reasoning behind the changes and how they benefit the sales people both short and long term. But you won't know what the worries are unless you ask, so always ask for feedback.

Set A Timeline For Communication

Communicating the new system will go a lot more smoothly if management agrees on a timeline before they start. Here's an effective one to try.

- Before sharing the new system, the head of sales sends out a message letting people know that there are upcoming changes.

- Next, the sales manager sends out another communication explaining the big picture of the new system, without getting into the technical details. If all staff use the system, this can go to everyone. If different teams use a different system, communications will need to be more personalized by team.

- Now, each individual manager sends the full details of the scheme to each of their staff members. Again, depending whether the team uses one scheme or different ones, communications need to be tweaked so that each staff member gets only the information relevant to them.

- The next step is a discussion about the new scheme with each staff member, where managers explain the technicalities and answer questions.
- A few days after this, have an open group session where people can air their concerns and put forward questions.
- Distribute the FAQ document built out of this discussion.
- And finally, make sure there is someone on hand to provide support and answer questions as the new scheme is put into place.

A Conclusion

A new sales scheme marks a big change in a company, but it also brings with it new possibilities and the potential for better revenue – something managers and sales staff can both appreciate. The key to communicating about the new scheme is to plan the communication properly and give it time and attention. Always make sure sales staff know why the new scheme matters to them, and make sure they have all the information and support they need to implement it with minimal problems.

Afterword

Fortunately, compensation and incentives plans work. They are tested and used by many companies around the globe, among different industries. As long as there is a field sales force in an institution, such programs will prevail. The two main reasons for their existence, the alignment of sales people to the sales strategy of the company and the motivation of the sales force to reach and outperform their targets, are valid. Not only real business cases from institutions of various sizes and industries around the globe but also experts in the field testify that sales compensation schemes work.

The problem however starts when these plans are poorly designed, when stakeholders put together a few terms and they call it a sales compensation plan and when such plans are designed within a short time without taking into account various aspects and processes, areas we have thoroughly analysed in this book. We have extensively mentioned a few consequences a poorly designed scheme has to the company and to the sales force.

The problem in the design process is not in the specific terms and conditions that one decided to use. It is not the decision of using a commission of five percent versus a commission of ten percent. It is not the decision to give a target of one or two hundred thousand dollars. The problem starts when one doesn't take into account that the process of designing a sales compensation plan contains various important steps, it starts far before deciding the terms and conditions and finishes a way after concluding with the design.

This book is intended exactly for this reason. To help companies to design an effective sales compensation plan that motivates sales people to sell beyond their targets. The white papers in this book are collated together in that way to present the process to follow in designing a scheme. The purpose of this book is a close guidance for the sales management and the team that is responsible to design the program. It can be used as a check list against the individual elements a program shall contain and the specific decisions that need to be made.

This book is touching upon every aspect of the design process analysing every single part of it. I would like to stress once more here that a program does not stop only to the quantitative part of it, deciding its terms and conditions. As I presented in the book, there are peripheral and additional areas equally important to the quantitative part that the owner of the scheme shall take into account.

INDEX

Resources, Bibliography And Notes

There was a constant sourcing of material, knowledge and subject matter expertise allowing me to finish this book. A substantial part of the resources is by personal experience working with companies of various industries and help them design an effective sales compensation program. Through advising sales management and compensation professionals, the flow of the design process had to be readjusted many times to include additional important sections and notions.

Great answers and valuable resources were found though in literature noted below that offered valuable insights in the subject.

Albrecht, Chad & Marley, Steve; "The Future of Sales Compensation", ZS Associates, Inc. Kindle Edition. ISBN: 978-0-9853436-6-8

Cichelli, David J.; "Compensating the Sales Force: A Practical Guide to Designing Winning Sales Reward Programs", Second Edition Kindle Edition, McGraw Hill Education

Colletti, Jerome; "Designing Sales Compensation Plans", WorldatWork

Colletti, Jerome; "Sales Compensation Math", WorldatWork

Colt, Stockton B. Jr; "The Sales Compensation Handbook", ISBN 0814404111

Dimisa, Joseph; "Sales compensation made simple", WorldatWork

Donnolo, Mark; "What Your CEO Needs to Know About Sales Compensation", AMACOM. Kindle Edition. ISBN: 978-0-8144-3228-0 (eBook)

Lopez, Federico; "Sales Compensation: A theoretical and practical methodology for designing and implementing Sales Incentive Plans for the Sales Force"

MacLean, Randy; "Profit-Driven Sales Commissions", ISBN 9781508502432

Nelson, Bob.; "1501 Ways to Reward Employees", Workman Publishing Company. Kindle Edition. ISBN: 978-0-9853436-6-8

Stockton B. Colt Jr.; "Sales Compensation A collection of articles from WorldatWork", WorldatWork

Zoltners, Andris; "Sales Compensation Solutions: Addressing the Toughest Sales Incentive Issues in Today's Changing World", ZS Associates, Inc. Kindle Edition. ISBN: 978-0-9989347-0-9

ZOLTNERS, Andris A; "The Complete Guide to Sales Force Incentive Compensation: How to Design and Implement Plans That Work", AMACOM. Kindle Edition. ISBN-10: 0-8144-7324-5

The below list of websites has been a continuous source of resources and knowledge in the matter.

Chartered Institute of Personnel and Development; www.cipd.co.uk

Industry Dive; www.hrdive.com

Recognition Professionals International; www.recognition.org

Incentive Research Foundation; www.theirf.org

WorldatWork Total Rewards Association; www.worldatwork.com

Copyright

ISBN: 978-1-8381616-0-6 (ebook)

ISBN: 978-1-8381616-1-3

ISBN: 978-1-8381616-2-0

First Edition

www.comp4sales.com by C4S Consultants Limited

Made in the USA
Middletown, DE
09 June 2022

66915550R00136